The Seven Wonders of the World

Text by Artur Müller

Photographs by Rolf Ammon

Introduction by Michael Grant

The Seven Wonders of the World

Five thousand years of
Culture and History in
the Ancient World

Translated by David Ash

McGraw-Hill Book Company

New York

© 1966 Scherz Verlag
München Bern Wien
English translation and introduction ©
Weidenfeld and Nicolson Ltd
Layout by A. Stankowski

All photographs are by
Rolf Ammon with the
exception of
P. 18/9: NASA photograph 65/H/1137
P. 55: British Museum, London
P. 282/3: State Museums, Berlin

The translation of the epigram attributed to
Antipater of Sidon (p. 188) has been published
by kind permission of the Right Reverend
William Philbin, Bishop of Down and Connor.

Library of Congress Catalog Card Number: 68–16684
43956
Printed and bound in Switzerland

Contents

Introduction by Michael Grant

Classical Greece was not very self-conscious about nature, or travelling, or sight-seeing. But all that changed enormously in the time of the massive monarchies which succeeded Alexander the Great. Geography books were written in a new scientific spirit, and this was also an age of deliberate and determined tourism. Travel-literature, which in old Ionian times had been of a practical or navigational nature, now blossomed forth into guide-books; the preservative Egyptian soil at Hawara has yielded up a papyrus which is one of them, and another bears the double name of Callicrates and Menecles, two unknowns who were perhaps the Baedekers of this Hellenistic world.

Polemon, who was born in the second century BC at the little town which was descended from Troy, ingeniously catered both for those with antiquarian preferences and for people who had a taste for the bizarre; he was nicknamed 'the hoarder of inscriptions', and yet he also wrote a book *On Marvels*. But the Greeks, with their keen sense of the ridiculous, had already for some time been making fun of this new fashion and passion. For example, an ancient Baron Münchausen, Antiphanes of Berge, produced a collection of tales about foreign parts which could scarcely be regarded as anything but incredible. One of his stories describes a country which is so cold that in autumn men's words freeze in the air, becoming audible when the thaw comes in the following spring. Accordingly 'Bergean' came to be the term for these fictitious accounts of a bogus geographical character. Their most

famous and amusing exponent was the Greco-Syrian satirist Lucian, who in Roman times parodied the whole of this sort of popular literature in his *True Story* which is full of outrageous travellers' tales.

But fake marvels were not enough for these people of the world which Alexander had so greatly expanded. Many people wanted not only to have their imagination titillated by tall stories but to learn about the marvels that really existed – and if possible to see them. For this was now much more practicable than it ever had been under the old warring city-states, since the new monarchies, although they fought against one another, nevertheless also maintained a general level of orderliness and security which made travelling possible over vast areas. And so, in about the middle of the third century BC, if not earlier, arose the idea of Great Sights to be seen. How many of them were there to be? The accepted answer was seven, and the authors of this book are right to make play with the talismanic quality of this number. Besides, it was large enough to comprise a good deal of information, and yet small enough to bring visits to every one of them within the bounds of a lifetime's possibility. The Seven Sights developed into the Seven Wonders of the World, which have passed so firmly into the culture and folklore of the ages that they are even listed in *Whitaker's Almanack* – where they appear between more modern informative titbits, The Largest Cities of the World and The World's Lakes.

Whitaker's list is the one which has passed into traditional usage. Yet I defy any reader to name all Seven

Wonders straight off: most people break down after three or four. That is one of a number of reasons why the present book was well worth writing. Moreover, quite apart from the more recent additions and substitutions to the list, of which Artur Müller will say something later on, the ancients themselves were not always in complete agreement about its contents. Indeed, there are said to be no less than twenty-five versions. For instance, a poetical epigram, which may or may not have been written by Antipater of Sidon (William Philbin, Bishop of Down and Connor, is to be thanked for the version printed on p.188), missed out the Lighthouse (*Pharos*) of Alexandria, and included instead the city walls of Babylon. Yet, imposing though they were, there was a certain inelegance about their selection, because the other items cover a wide geographical and cultural range, whereas the inclusion of the walls means that Babylon gets two items out of seven. So in came the Pharos instead. The other Wonders are as follows: – The Pyramids; the Hanging Gardens of Babylon; the Zeus of Phidias at Olympia; the Temple of Artemis at Ephesus; the Mausoleum of Halicarnassus; and the Colossus of Rhodes.

Later on the Romans managed to insert the Colosseum also. This insertion not only provided a fitting verbal echo of the Colossus, but the repeated emphasis on the colossal recalls a significant point. We often like to dwell on the fact that the classical Greeks had a fastidious taste for small-scale perfection – and it is true that they produced exquisite vases, coins and gems.

But what even they most admired, as will be seen, was the vast and glittering Zeus of Olympia. The later, Hellenistic Greeks (the same is even more conspicuously true of the Romans) found hugeness very particularly appealing, and it is not fortuitous that each of the Seven Wonders was enormous.

Sheer size is a matter of quality as well as quantity, and changes values. What Julian Huxley said about living organisms is just as true of buildings and other works of art: – 'Simply magnify an object without changing its shape, and, without meaning to, you have changed all its properties.' Gazing at a gigantic temple at Baalbek, Sir Mortimer Wheeler considered the same point. 'Imagine a *little* Empire State Building, bereft of the size and vista that give some sort of status, I suppose, to the actual pile; the thought horrifies. Imagine a *little* St Peter's, such as can in fact be seen somewhere in Canada. . . . Look at a little pyramid; a big pyramid has to fight hard enough for intelligent recognition, but those *little* pyramids that the Pharaonic builders did not hesitate to scatter round and about are surely silly toys beyond belief.'

Whether it has to fight for recognition or not – and certainly it is not always readily classifiable as a work of art – there is at least no doubt about the bigness of the Pyramid of Cheops; this is, indeed, a glimpse of the obvious, like a long-since unfashionable sentimental song called 'London is so big'. But London is many buildings and the Pyramid one, and this single Pyramid is believed to consist of as many as 2,300,000 separate blocks. If these were sawn into one-foot cubes which were then lined up in a single file, they would stretch two-thirds of the way round the world at the equator. The Great Pyramid lost its casing of Tura limestone, but remained for nearly five thousand years the highest building in the world, yet only one hundred years before it existed there were no large stone buildings in Egypt – or anywhere else in the world.

So much for the idea that ancient Egyptian civilisation was always timeless and unchangeable. This was evolution at an almost inconceivably rapid pace. But what makes the imagination reel is the combination of these dimensions with an almost terrifying degree of constructional precision – to the nearest one-fiftieth or sometimes even one-hundredth of an inch. It is fashionable nowadays, and I believe it is right, to say that the earliest Egyptian dynasties and the pre-dynastic periods before them owed a great deal to the already highly evolved cultures of southern Mesopotamia – and for such reasons many modern geographers like to treat the Mediterranean and the whole near east as a single area.

Yet, as so often, the pupils outdid their masters. The Egyptians had access to the stone which the Mesopotamians lacked, and a pyramid was always ten times as impressive as those not altogether dissimilar Sumerian objects known as Ziggurats, such as the Tower of Babel. Although it is hazardous to discuss why they were built, and how they came to be built in this way, the purpose of the two types of building was probably much the same: to bring the ruler nearer to heaven, and heaven nearer to the ruler. Of the Ziggurats Herodotus wrote, 'The Chaldaeans say (but I do not believe them) that the god himself is wont to visit the shrine and rest upon the couch', and Texts relating to the Egyptian Pyramids include a magic spell proclaiming that 'a staircase to heaven is laid for the ruler so that he may mount up to heaven thereby'.

The rulers, the Pharaohs, were apparently the first men in the whole of human history to reign over an entire country. For Egypt, made one because of its exceptional geographical position and unique unifying factor the Nile, had become the first large-scale nation-state anywhere in the world. It was natural for its monarchs to worship the life-giving, light-giving, fertilising Sun (only an Ethiopian tribe, where the climate was hotter still, considered it a torrid Devil). At the other, latest extremity of ancient history the same Sun-worship took over the Roman court, and would very probably have taken over the Roman world if Constantine had not decided to supersede it, at first partially and then wholly, by Christianity.

'Pyramid' is the Greek word for wheat-cake, and according to one theory, which is very likely to be correct, the name was first given these structures by irreverent visiting Greek traders or mercenaries, in the same jocular spirit in which they named other sun-worshipping monuments 'obelisks', or little skewers. However, the two words do at least now convey to us a clear meaning. The name 'Hanging Gardens of Babylon', on the other hand – which stands for the second

Wonder of the World – is misleading. 'Hanging' may be the literal equivalent of the Greek *kremastos* or the Latin *pensilis*, but the Gardens only hung in the air in the sense that they consisted of superimposed layers of terraces, upon the roof of Nebuchadnezzar's great palace. On each terrace there was a layer of mould so deep that it provided soil for the most lavish vegetation, including even fruit-trees. Underneath the mould, to protect the roofs and ceilings of the royal apartments below, were thick sheets of lead, and rushes, and the local bitumen which Mesopotamians made use of before they ever exploited their oil. Yet now it needs a portentous feat of mental reconstruction to conjure up all those masses of tropical verdure, and the water which cunningly irrigated them. 'Picture,' wrote J.A.Brendon in the expansive style of a more leisurely archaeological generation, 'these lofty terraces, their many arches festooned with flowering creepers, and all the platforms ablaze with the most gorgeously scented and coloured flowers which Asia – indeed, the then known world – could produce, shaded from the too hot sun by trees laden in their seasons with rich and luscious fruits. Picture, in this paradise of sybaritic and Oriental luxury, in the heart of great Babylon, the Median queen holding her splendid court.' Try to picture all this, indeed, in the dusty Iraqi wilderness. It is true that a good bit of the foundations of the Hanging Gardens of Babylon still remains to be seen – if, indeed, that is the right identification for the remains of irrigation works which one of the three ancient mounds has disclosed. However, by a gloomy, if inevitable, destiny the impermanent greenery has gone, and these skeletons of what appear to be terraces and once-vaulted chambers, eked out by modern supports, seem to add to the blinding heat instead of any longer beguiling it away.

Yet it is significant of the power and efficiency of Nebuchadnezzar that there is evidence for the extensive use of stone. For this was a country where, as Professor Myers remarked, 'a stone door-socket was a rich gift of a king to his god, and was rescued from one ruin after another, to be reused and proudly rededicated'. If, as seems probable, stone was employed abundantly in a stone-less land, this is as remarkable, in its way, as the many-ton blocks of the Pyramids, in the limestone country of Egypt. It underlines the unbelievable feats of staff-work, transport and grinding labour which brought these regal monuments into existence.

If the remains of the Gardens have been rightly identified, let us frankly admit that, however much they inspired Greeks to include them among the Seven Wonders of the World, these lumps of rubble are depressing for all but the most fanatical and clairvoyant and thirst-impervious tourist. Indeed, how often, not only here but elsewhere as well, does the antiquarian-minded tourist have to keep his imagination working overtime! Almost everything has changed so vastly from what it was. And this is even the case when there is a good deal still on view – far more than at Babylon. What an effort it is, for example, at Rome, to imagine those great ugly masses of brick and concrete back into the elegant though giant-sized luxury of the Baths of Caracalla! Ancient history, for that reason, is quite a different sort of study from modern history. Our evidence is lost, or fragmentary, or ill-balanced, or – in the case of literature – heavily biased, for or against.

By the same token, the material remains associated with the ancient potentates have been transformed or have crumbled to such an extent that a great deal of creative, imaginative research has to get to work before they mean anything to us. Yet, that, after all, is one of the chief reasons why the study of the ancient world is tantalising, fascinating, absorbing. It is totally different, by its very nature, from the study of more recent times. Its disciplines are both harder and different. Yet they must be faced, not only because they are so challenging but because the modern world can only be understood by knowing what has gone before.

A classic example of these tantalising disappearances and destructions is provided by the third Wonder of the World, the statue of Zeus carved by Phidias in *c.* 438–432 BC for his great temple at Olympia. For this has vanished altogether. It is true that the museum at Olympia preserves some of the greatest masterpieces in the world: sculpture from the pediments and metopes of a few decades earlier, and the later Hermes of Praxiteles. But the Zeus is not among them. It may have been plundered on the spot when the temple went out of use in Christian times; though according to another tradition it was taken off to Constantinople and destroyed there in a fire. Anyway, it has disappeared. Only its position

in the temple is still marked by fragments of the blue marble that formed its base. In order to discover what it was like, our detective talents have to be exercised to the utmost. We have a representation of the statue on a coin. But the coin dates from over half a millennium later, is not very brilliantly executed, and only gives a rather schematic picture.

So this does not help very much in assessing or explaining the profound, not to say shattering, effect which this statue of Zeus quite evidently exercised upon its beholders. The figure appealed to intellectuals as well as religious people, and the philosopher Epictetus remarked that it was a misfortune to die without having seen it. Later in this book it will be possible to read how another perceptive Greek of the same Roman period, Dion Chrysostom of Prusa, tried to sum up what this Zeus represented. And Dion also commented, 'I feel that any man of heavy heart, bowed beneath a load of misfortune and grief, who had lost even the solace of sleep, if he stood before this statue of the god, would cast aside his troubles and the sorrows that befall us all.'

Even a Roman general, Aemilius Paullus, was stirred by the evident presence of divinity. The literary critic Quintilian made the interesting observation that the beauty of the image may be said to have added something to the received religion. This is not too hard to appreciate, because a great sculptural conception (as we can see from the Apollo which still survives in the Olympia Museum) discloses more clearly than a hundred textbooks what ancient Greek religion was all about.

The Apollo belongs to the borderline and turning-point between late archaic severity and the full flood of Greek classicism. The Zeus, on the other hand, represented the very epitome of that latter, classical age, with its strange blend of idealism and close observation, which emerges most clearly from the artistic masterpieces of Athens. Yet the Zeus of Phidias would also, surely, shock us out of some of our preconceived ideas about that age, lovingly handed on by modern educational systems. I have already mentioned our unwillingness to recognise the Greek taste for the colossal; and this was forty feet high. A worse shock still would have been the statue's rich and flashing colour. Not only was it seated upon a gold-plated, painted, engraved throne inlaid with ebony, semi-precious stones and glass, but the figure itself (which was of wood) had its flesh parts covered by sheets of ivory – enormous numbers of them, since no piece of ivory is very large – while the drapery was picked out by glittering plates of solid gold. Nothing less spectacular seemed worthy of the greatest statues of the greatest deities; though the point was long evaded by people of later ages who liked to see in the Greeks a delicate faded refinement – as well as a successful pursuit of the Rational Mean which, in reality, they admired so much precisely because they realised how far from this achievement so many of their proceedings were.

If, on the other hand, it seems to us that such lavishly colourful, expensive grandeur might betray an oriental origin, we should be right. This 'chryselephantine' tech-nique can now be identified in Minoan Crete, where recently discovered portions of ivory statuettes are found to have been partially covered with gold leaf. And from Crete the technique can be traced back to the ivory work that flourished most greatly and abundantly in the cities of the Levant. As our horizons of antiquity extend, the number and variety of the themes and motifs and methods which Greece borrowed from the near east become clearer and clearer. Yet, having received these and absorbed their inspiration, she transformed them totally. And there, in that combination of borrowing with extreme originality, lies the essence of the classical miracle.

Nowhere can this blend have been more notable than in the fourth Wonder of the World, the temple of Artemis (Diana) at Ephesus. For Ephesus (Selçuk) was situated on the Anatolian coast – which has now receded – at the end of the great Asian trade-route, and of all Greek cities it was the most exposed to eastern civilisations. Under their influence it helped to perfect the Ionic architectural style, of which this huge shrine was one of the archetypes.

The temple cannot easily be thought of as standing for a single period or cultural phase, since its story ran richly through one age after another. The cult of this Artemis was of extreme antiquity, for she was related to the mother-goddess who linked Greece with the remote and non-Greek past. Weird statues of the Ephesian goddess – so different from the classical huntress Diana – have their shapeless bodies cluttered with a host of symbols and emblems, of which the most alarming are those multiple pendant objects that used to be interpreted as breasts but are now considered to be eggs, unless you prefer to regard them as dates. The cult long preceded any temple; the earliest known building was of the seventh century BC, and a more sensational structure was erected just over a century later – with the help of king Croesus of Lydia, who thus bears witness to those eastern connections in which Ephesus specialised. Nothing of such a size had ever been seen before, and indeed there was a conscious intention of exceeding Hera's temple at Samos. Yet the temple of Artemis seen by Hellenistic tourists was another one again, built after a fourth-century fire which was followed by the Ephesians' tactful, successful effort to prevent Alexander from inscribing his name on the façade. And this temple seemed to Antipater of Sidon the greatest Wonder of all. Outside Mount Olympus, he said, the Sun has never seen its like.

But of these unprecedentedly sumptuous buildings the modern tourist will find little or nothing more than he has found of Zeus's statue at Olympia. Or, to be exact, he will find, on a bare and sometimes soggy piece of ground, a few mutilated chunks of column. Here, indeed, is food for those thoughts of the transience of man which have given us, farther west, so many fine seventeenth- and eighteenth-century landscapes showing overgrown ruins: except that on the site of the Ephesus shrine it is hard to find anything to overgrow. To be fair, there is still a lot to see round about, but of the temple there is virtually nothing.

Its site was found in the nineteenth century by the heroic Mr J.T.Wood, architect and builder of railways. 'Six years,' Freya Stark tells us, 'he worked in a frock-coat and pork-pie hat through the malarian summers, while a devoted and (luckily) well-to-do wife distributed quinine to the peasants – until the temple was found.' Later a trained archaeologist, D.G.Hogarth, made an equally intrepid attack, and discovered three thousand objects, including a hoard of jewellery and ivory statuettes. He dug down to the lowest foundation through water and slime, and his book *A Wandering Scholar in the Levant* (1896) gives an enthralling account of the hardships, disappointments and rewards of an excavator's life.

But for sheer excitement and drama there is nothing to compare with the nineteenth chapter of *The Acts of Apostles*. This tells in detail how St Paul encountered the religious and financial interests that were vested in this temple. 'So that not only,' said one of its silver-smiths, 'is our craft in danger to be set at nought; but also that the temple of the great goddess Diana should be despised, and her magnificence should be destroyed, whom all Asia and the world worshippeth. . . .' And then, 'all with one voice about the space of two hours cried out "Great is Diana of the Ephesians!"' And Paul was lucky to escape alive.

Of the spectacular tomb of Mausolus, the original Mausoleum, at Halicarnassus (Bodrum) in the south-western corner of Asia Minor there is another sad tale of non-survival to tell. 'Reaching the site where the Mausoleum itself once stood, we came into the garden of a tweed-capped peasant, who regarded us with blank indifference. We ferreted around in the rank, dry weeds, hoping to find at least some fragment of stone which might once have graced part of the tomb, but in vain. Where a Wonder of the World once reared its fabulous head, nothing now remains but this unkempt garden, planted with vegetable marrows and a few ragged fig-trees, enjoying an agreeable view of the sea.' The traveller is Lord Kinross, and the reason why he could find nothing was because earlier visitors from the west, the knights of St John of Jerusalem, had demolished the building four centuries ago.

Later, a century or so ago, C.T. Newton and the British Navy removed some precious marbles from the site – with the permission of the Sultan of Ottoman Turkey. They are now in the British Museum. In some countries (notably Greece) such removals during the last century are a delicate topic, causing from time to time strained political relations. Should the marbles have stayed where they were? But if so would they have survived? Yet ought they now to be returned? Is every country going to return to every other country all that has been taken from it? Unlikely. And even if it happened, would that not make all museums (and picture galleries) very parochial? Where should one draw the line?

At all events the British Museum has substantial parts of the Mausoleum's frieze, and the two statues which are likewise illustrated in this book. The female figure, believed to represent Queen Artemisia, has lost her head, but the man, who is surely her husband (and brother) king Mausolus himself, has kept his; and its style is significant. Not only is this a leading masterpiece of the fourth century BC, which so subtly and sophisticatedly modified and softened fifth-century classicism, but the face looks very un-Greek. And indeed Mausolus *was* un-Greek; he was what the Greeks called a barbarian – a man of Caria, who like thousands of other Asians had become imbued with some Greek civilisation, and aspired to more.

A few decades later Alexander the Great, himself belonging to outlying Macedonia where the rulers exemplified the same tendency, was to spread this process over enormous territories of the east. Although he used force, the cultural commodity he had to offer (like modern technology) was in considerable demand; the evidence comes from people like Mausolus, whose Hellenisation was not compulsory but spontaneous. And it was precisely in Mausolus' time that the Athenian philosopher, orator and educationalist Isocrates, apostle of a pan-Hellenism intended to overcome city-state narrowness, proclaimed that to be a Greek was a matter not of race but of upbringing and training.

The survival of statues and reliefs from the Mausoleum gives it an unusual quality among the Seven Wonders, for, in general, one of the most conspicuous features of these once-famous sights is their total non-existence today. And that, indeed, is one of the things that makes them useful, since it means that the list of Wonders leads us conveniently and unerringly to extremely important masterpieces of which we should otherwise have little knowledge. A further instance of this is provided by Chares' famous statue of the Sun (Helios) known as the Colossus of Rhodes. And here we have, in addition, a notorious fable and misunderstanding to contend with. On Rhodes today – that island, for some reason, although many other islands are charming too, peculiarly favoured and singled out by Scandinavian tourists – the postcards for sale displaying the Colossus still show him bestriding the harbour as depicted, in accordance with a medieval fable, by the Austrian Fischer von Erlach (1656–1723). But the statue had never, in fact, done anything of the kind. We do not quite know exactly where it stood, but though it was very large (105 feet high) it was certainly normal in its pose and did nothing so un-Greek as the splits.

Yet the interest of Fischer von Erlach, one of the greatest baroque masters, was understandable, for this Greek art of the third century BC had possessed many qualities which were ancestral to the baroque. Rhodes had been one of the principal artistic workshops of these Hellenistic styles. The centuries that followed Alexander were the age not only of great monarchies, but of the extraordinary little naval, mercantile, island city-state of Rhodes, which (until it made the mistake of enlisting the help of Rome) stood for peace and trade and the security of the seas. One of the finest tributes earned

by any ancient community was received by Rhodes when a great deal of the city, including the Colossus, was knocked down by an earthquake in 225 BC. For, despite the self-seeking power politics of the age, all the leading kingdoms rallied round in order to help repair the damage, and so did many of the smaller states as well.

Yet Rhodes, although in many ways the most interesting phenomenon of those times, was eclipsed by another and far larger city. That was Alexandria, the symbol of the times as surely as Athens had been the leader of the classical epoch which had gone before. And the great new capital of the Ptolemies, made immortal again in our own century by its Greek poet Kavafy, was very soon itself symbolised by its Pharos, for which room had to be made among the Wonders of the World. Ancestor of many other lighthouses, it was indeed a startling creation, as the description at the end of this book will show – again with the help of detective work upon literary sources and coins.

In most cases – though the Pyramids form a conspicuous exception – these Wonders are no longer with us. But they are an integral and essential and legendary part of the human story, and, even today, no tourism of the ancient world could give a fair picture unless its peregrinations upon actual ruins were supplemented by some imaginative knowledge of these Seven Sights: seeing that these, however evasive to the modern sightseer their remains may be, were once classified as the greatest and most worthwhile objects of scrutiny and admiration in the whole of the known world.

In the Beginning was the
Number

When we look at modern cities by day and by night, miracles of organisation and technology, when we think of medical science clinically bringing the dead back to life, or the machines devised by man to work faster and more accurately than himself, or the aircraft that cross the entire globe like meteors, or the space capsules rocketing to the moon, then it is difficult for us to think at the same time of man as an animal, living among animals, or of man taking tens of thousands of years to shape the first tool out of stone, kindle the first fire and build the first cave dwelling with mud, sticks and stones. But when we note how modern man murders and makes war, how cruel and brutal he is, then the difference between man and the animals does not seem so great, even today, and we realise that man lives

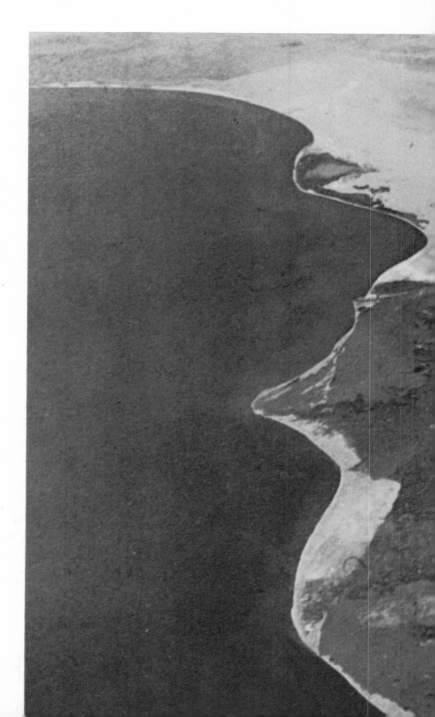

Space photograph of the Nile Delta, taken from Gemini IV in June 1965

18

according to laws that have been handed down from time immemorial.

Living and dying is the eternal theme: stars appear and burn themselves out, continents rise up and sink, civilisations emerge from the void, surround themselves with splendours, then vanish as if they had never been. 'All things are in a flux.' What once was great and seemed everlasting is today buried beneath the drifting sand. Like a bundle of tow in the fire, so earthly glory passes away.

But it is precisely for this reason that man searches the past for whatever has survived, big or small, fair or foul, for he loathes and dreads to think that he and all his works will fade away.

He conducts careful researches to find what remains and prove to himself that the chain of life is unbreakable. He tries to fathom out what happened in the history of men and their world. But this alone is not enough: he must also know why these things happened, and whether and in what way they are connected with events of the same period in other places. And secretly he hopes to deduce laws that will make him master over these events, and let him determine the course of history.

The history of the earth began about five hundred and forty million years ago. In the space of some three hundred million years there appeared plants, a few vertebrates, crabs, cartilaginous fishes and finally reptiles. In the next hundred and forty million years the giant saurians lived on the earth, the first birds evolved from the reptiles, mammals appeared, and the great

trees flourished. It took almost fifty-five million years for more mammals to develop to the point where the first anthropoid apes emerged, knowing fire and using bones and stones as tools. But not until the Ice Age, that is, between 600,000 and 10,000 BC, do we find man the cave-dweller, living by hunting and able to represent the world around him in art. His idol regards us with big round eyes, its face masked with a stag's head; it has the paws of a bear and a horse's tail.

The first man, the final stage in the story of the creation, is contained in every mythology and studied by every branch of science. Above man there is God, and he is distinguished by his direct relationship with Him. And God said: 'It is not good that man should be alone; I will make him an help meet for him.' And He created

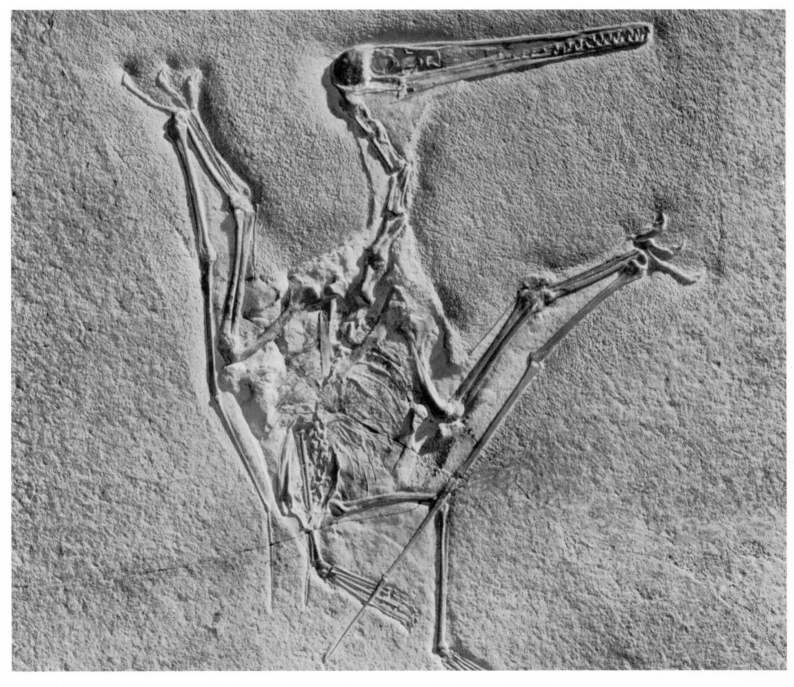

Homo sapiens – fossil remains of a male (left) and female (right) skull, 80,000–10,000 BC, found at Obercassel near Bonn, Germany (Anthropological Institute, Munich)
Opposite: Battle between gods and giants, from the frieze of the treasury of Siphnos at Delphi

woman for the first man out of man himself. To both He gave the commandment not to eat of the tree in the midst of the Garden of Eden, the tree of knowledge of good and evil, lest they die. Tempted by the cunning serpent, the woman took of the fruit of the tree of knowledge, and they both did eat. Now they stood between good and evil, between life and death, and their earthly life began, with its unceasing demands for decisions. So it is told to us in the Bible.

In Greek mythology, man grew out of the soil of the Earth Mother, who also bore the gods. And the offspring, gods and men, came together in fraternal strife. Prometheus, son of the Titans, stole fire from heaven and gave it to man. Whereupon Zeus swore to destroy mankind. Out of clay he shaped Pandora, the most beau-

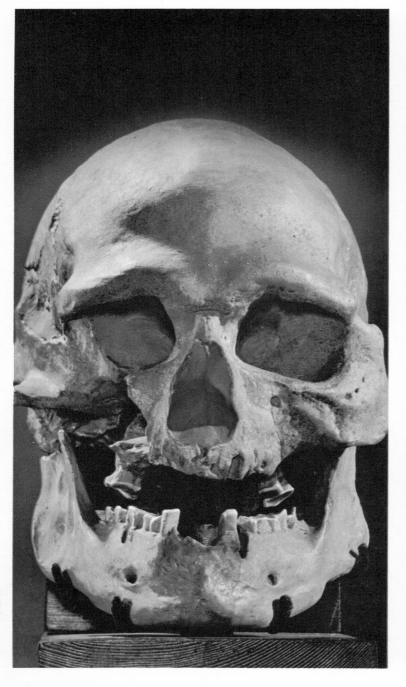

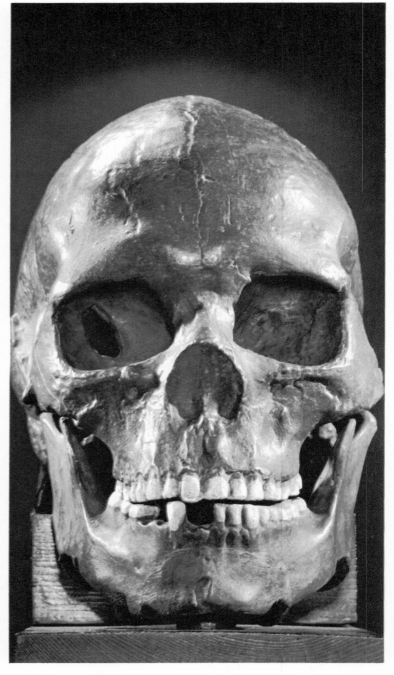

tiful woman ever created, and gave her a box that contained all the evils. And man received the woman and opened the mysterious gift of the gods. And so man's fate began. Plagued with illness, old age, madness, vice and passions, men sought the way back to their relationship with God. Abraham made a covenant with God, and in the new covenant this makes possible man's salvation through the Son of God and his self-sacrifice. The Greeks sought transformation and salvation through the Earth Mother, the great goddess, and the covenant of the mysteries.

Such is man's place on earth: between good and evil, war and peace, submission and defiance, heaven and hell, life and death. Sharing in the divine essence, he is at the same time its opposite extreme. He is a creator of truth and beauty, and at the same time destroyer of the godly world. Mankind's path is marked with beauty and splendour, but also with blood and tears. This path first becomes apparent and meaningful to us in Egypt, Mesopotamia and Central Asia. Here, in the third millennium BC, political and social life and cultural activity reached a first high point.

A second summit was reached by mankind in Egypt and Asia Minor in the second millennium BC. From the eighth to the sixth century BC the path of blood and splendour leads through Assyria and Persia to Greece. The world is born anew from man's will and imagination. The trail moves slowly across to Italy. From the first century BC to the first century AD, Rome brings together all of Western Europe and finally embraces the

whole of the then-known world in one empire. A century later, the creative power of the Old World has already begun to flag. The Teutons in the west and the Slavs in the east split up the Roman world into a Western and an Eastern Empire.

Nations and rulers vanished, the noblest products of art and culture were ruined, destroyed or totally annihilated. What has remained to this day is a vision of human and superhuman exertion, a memory of great heights of human culture and civilisation, and the knowledge that all subsequent human effort can be distinguished only in extent and never in essence from what was already once achieved in antiquity. Mankind can see that the developments of the past, those of an old and long-since vanished world, are also the developments of today. He

Left: 'Drunken old woman', third century BC (Glyptothek, Munich)
Right: 'Barberini faun', third century AD, found in 1624 during building work on the Castel Sant'Angelo, Rome (Glyptothek, Munich)
Opposite: Battle scene – a four-horse chariot with warriors – depicted on an Attic vase of about 530 BC (State Collections of Antiquities, Munich)

can recognise that people in every age are striving to push the same stone up the hill. The same stone: government by a central bureaucracy or a single individual in whose hands all the strings converge and whose fingers control the subjects as the rulers wish, or government of a sovereign people by their chosen representatives. And finally the attempt to join the free, autonomous states in one great federation and bring peace to the world.

From time and motion stem impermanence. From impermanence, the desire for continuance. From the desire for continuance, the wish for remembrance – for monuments. Just as the stars of the Pleiades, the seven heavenly daughters, are spread across the night-blue mantle of the sky, holding it in their grasp – the Pleiades that governed all work on the earth and the sea, and were the forebears of the great tribes of ancient heroes who in later generations determined the fate of the earth – so the Pleiad of the Seven Wonders of the Ancient World, the seven stars of man's creative power, held together the bond of time across thousands of years, and excited the desires and imagination of all succeeding generations.

Is the figure seven an accident, or a whim of mankind?

Pythagoras, native of Samos and 'wise as none of the mortals', taught that all things in heaven and earth are arranged in numerical proportion. This arose from the discovery that the pitch of a taut string varies exactly in inverse proportion to its length.

Reliable measurements have shown that the basic

proportions of acoustical harmony are built into the sacred buildings of the Greeks, and indeed may be found in all the sacred buildings of the ancient world.

Through the symmetry of the Golden Section and the holy number, the sacred building as a whole and in all its parts reflects the macrocosm. Its originator is therefore not man, but God himself.

Seven is the only number out of the first ten that is neither a factor nor a product of any of the others. For this reason it was called the virgin number and given the name of the virgin Pallas Athene, who, having sprung from the head of Zeus, married neither god nor man: the enclosed and encircled, complete and consummate number, symbol of divinity that never alters though it brings change to nature and human life.

Opposite: Pharaoh with subject peoples, a painted relief from the temple of Ptah at Memphis (Cairo Museum)
Right: King Darius battling with a demon – a relief on a door-stone of the palace of Darius at Persepolis

Seven planets, ruled by seven princes, circle the sun in fixed orbits.

The seven-layered retina of the eye is a physical expression of the way in which the figure seven is reflected in the spiritual and material world.

Seven steps in the shape of a pyramid support the tomb of Cyrus the Great of Persia, King of Kings.

There are seven parts making up the oldest Egyptian pyramid in the burial ground at Saqqara.

Seven satraps, chosen from the seven most powerful families in Persia, ruled over the seven provinces of the empire.

And twice seven nations are depicted on the imperial palace at Persepolis, grouped round the enthroned King of Kings.

The imperial and temple cities of Babylon, Jerusalem and Rome stood on seven hills.

Symbol of the eternal light reflected by the seven planets, the seven-branched candlestick stood in the temple of Jehovah.

For seven times seven years, Athens sent seven youths and seven maidens to King Midas's labyrinth, with its seven enclosures, in atonement for the whole nation. But the Athenian hero Theseus, who performed seven deeds for the liberation and glorification of his country, sailed to Crete with seven pairs of Ionian youths and put an end to the horror. Seven heroes of Greece set out under Theseus's command against seven-gated Thebes to restore the exiled Polynices to his rightful throne. It is consequently no surprise that the Greeks of the sixth

century BC held up as their models the Seven Wise Men: Thales, Pittacus, Bias, Solon, Cleobulus, Chilon and Periander.

As to seven 'astounding sights', there was already an established list in ancient times. They were:

The three Great Pyramids of Egypt, built between 2,700 and 2,600 BC.

The Hanging Gardens of Semiramis at Babylon, laid out by King Nebuchadnezzar II, who reigned from 605 to 562 BC.

The Ivory and Gold Statue of Zeus at Olympia, the work of the Attic sculptor Phidias during the period of about 435 to 420 BC.

The Temple of Artemis at Ephesus, built after 365 BC on the foundations of the first temple, destroyed by fire.

The Mausoleum at Halicarnassus, a monument to the Carian prince Mausolus, built by order of his wife in about 350 BC and after.

The Colossus of Rhodes, a gigantic bronze statue of the god Helios, erected between 300 and 280 BC.

Finally, dating from about the same period, the Pharos of Alexandria, the archetype of all lighthouses, built during the reign of the Ptolemies in Egypt.

It was in about 250 BC that the first list appeared of Τὰ Ἑπτὰ Θεάματα, later called 'The Seven Wonders of the Ancient World'. The original has not been preserved. The later lists – in all about twenty-five have been handed down from antiquity – all derive from the first, however. One or two items vary. Thus, in place of the Hanging Gardens of Babylon, it is more common to

Top left: The Mausoleum at Halicarnassus, engraving by Fischer von Erlach (British Museum Library, London)
Top right: The Colossus of Rhodes, engraving by Fischer von Erlach (British Museum Library, London)
Right: The Pharos of Alexandria, engraving by Fischer von Erlach (British Museum Library, London)

Below: The step pyramid of King Zoser at Saqqara, seen from the south-west
Bottom: The tomb of King Cyrus the Great at Pasargardae
Opposite: Statue of Apollo, copy of a vanished original of the second century BC (British Museum, London)
Overleaf: Persian king and attendant; the king is holding a phallic symbol. Detail from the right-hand stairway of the Apadana at Persepolis.

find the Walls of Babylon listed, or even both together, and the Pharos of Alexandria left out.

The Romans included the Amphitheatrum Flavium (the Roman Colosseum) in the list. And as knowledge of the structures themselves grew vaguer over the centuries, so the items listed became more fantastic and abstruse.

Then in the Renaissance the original tradition was brought to mind once more as part of the general rediscovery of antiquity. Great painters and draughtsmen such as Maerten van Heemskerck (1498–1574), Philip Galle (1537–1612) and Marten de Vos (1532–1603), to name only the most important, now sought to reconstruct them pictorially. Imagination still played a very large part in their efforts. The famous baroque

master-builder Johann Bernhard Fischer von Erlach (1656–1723) was the first to take the descriptions given by the ancient authors and incorporate them with the greatest possible accuracy in his reconstructions, and he set out the results in his *Entwurff einer Historischen Architectur* ('Outline for a Historical Architecture'), first published in Vienna in 1721. Although no archaeological-historical discoveries were at that time available to him – such research began only in the nineteenth century – these actually confirmed how accurate part of his work had been.

From time to time, classical scholars have proposed new Wonders of the World from among still-existing buildings in place of those that have disappeared – for instance, the porcelain pagoda in Nanking, the Great Wall of China, the Hagia Sophia in Constantinople, the Leaning Tower of Pisa, the catacombs of Alexandria, or Stonehenge in England. But the list of the Seven Wonders of the Ancient World, which itself dates back to ancient days, is not affected by this.

Classifying the visible traces of vanished peoples of a particular period, explaining the function and significance of objects, uncovering the secrets of morphogenesis – such is the task and problem of archaeology. Its ultimate aim is thereby to reveal plainly to us the political, social and religious life of the men who made these things.

Among the various visible traces of the past, archaeologists recognise different categories of remains.

Most important of these are fixed remains, that is,

buildings. As far as cultural development is concerned, this means above all religious buildings.

Secular buildings form the second category of fixed remains. These include city walls and gates, private houses and public squares that provided the setting for general trading activities and political gatherings among the townspeople. Also included are public facilities for physical training, education and competitive games in Greece, such as stadiums, running-tracks, palaestras and gymnasiums; spas, cisterns, inns, hotels which, like the Leonidaeum at Olympia, accommodated visitors to the great religious and sports festivals. The palaces of kings, which served both as dwelling-places and as symbols of the power of the state, must also be mentioned. Other secular buildings include the tombs of

Below: The god Ahuramazda – a relief at Persepolis
Opposite: The goddess Athena, detail from the paintings on a water-vase from Attica, about 530 BC (Glyptothek, Munich)

the great rulers and the theatres in Greece, which remind us, however, that no building serving worldly functions was unconnected with religion and worship.

The large sculptures of the ancient Oriental empires, Greece and the Hellenic world – single figures and groups of gods, men and beasts of which hardly any still stand in their original location, but are dispersed throughout museums the world over – form the second group of archaeological remains.

The third group comprises the reliefs – originally painted, like the statues – that we find ranging through every period in Egypt, Babylonia, Assyria, Persia, Asia Minor and Greece.

The fourth group of archaeological remains includes works classed among the minor arts, a description which

Below: Tomb of Cleobulus on a small island opposite the acropolis of Lindus on the island of Rhodes
Opposite: 'Field of shards' on the site of the Old Babylonian city of Ishchali to the north-east of Baghdad

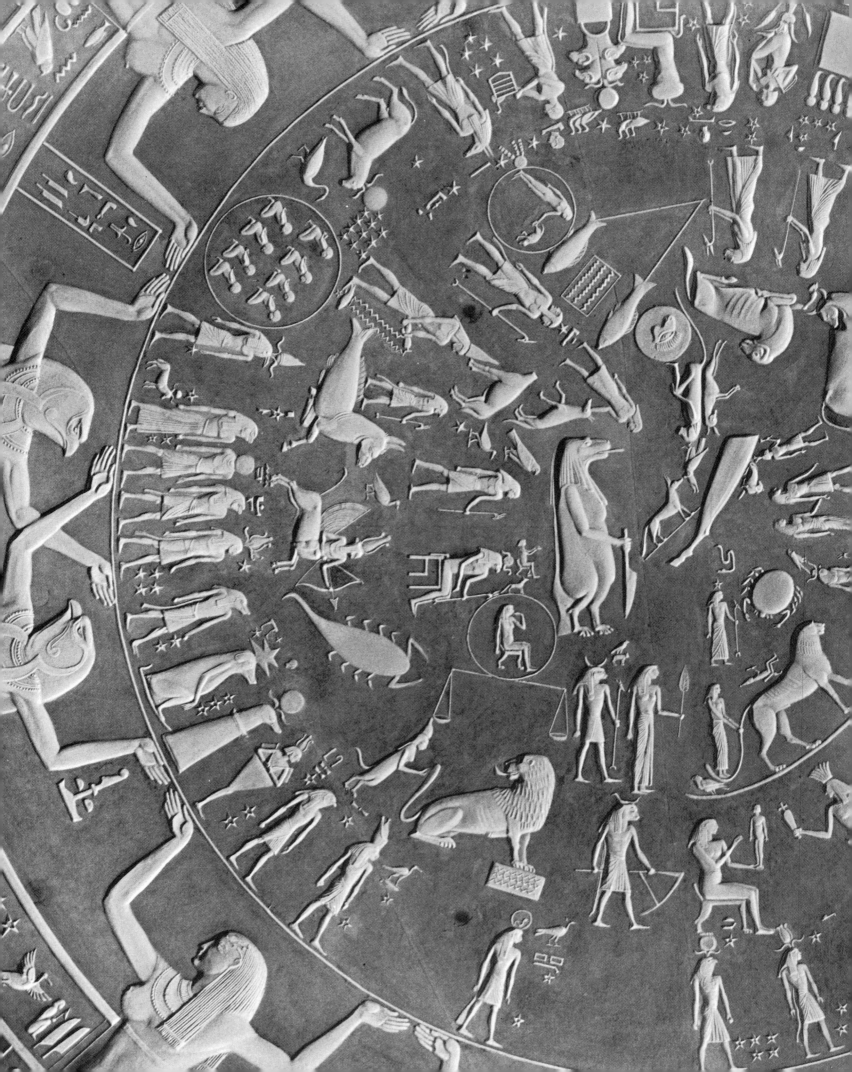

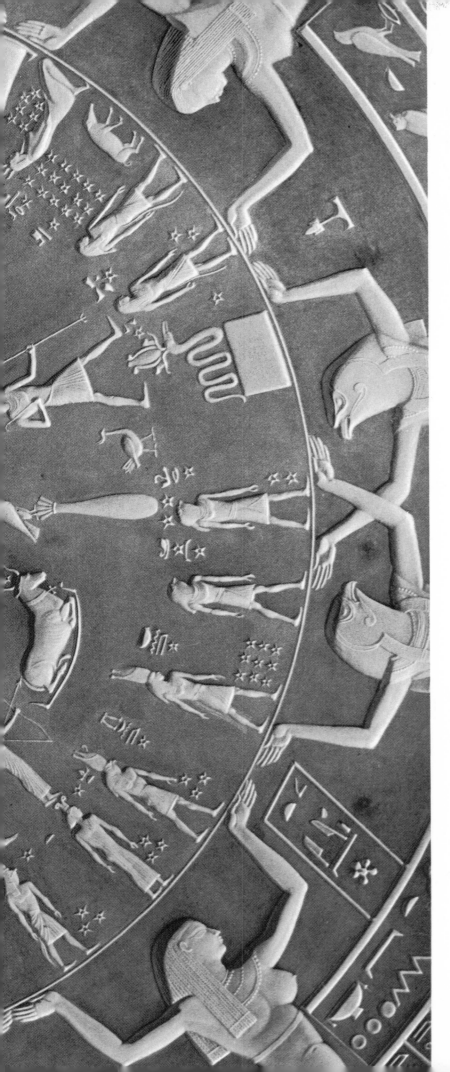

refers only to their size and not their importance. These include bronze statuettes, terracottas and items in everyday use. The art of pottery – ceramics – has a predominant place among the minor arts, for without its products thousands of years of prehistory and ancient history would remain completely obscure to us.

The age, variety and special characteristics of ceramics enable archaeologists to separate different cultures and periods.

The pictures on Greek vases give at least an idea of the manner of painting in many different periods where the major works are completely lost.

Coins, beginning with those of the Greek cities of Asia Minor from the seventh century BC, make up the fifth group of remains. These enable archaeologists to

Symbolic representation of the Egyptian zodiac from the temple of Hathor at Dendera (Louvre, Paris)

41

Left: Palm grove near the temple of Ptah at Memphis
Below: Landscape in Kurdistan, near Behistun in Iran

compile accurate chronologies, identify historical figures, reconstruct ruined buildings, locate surviving sculptures or, with the aid of literary sources, obtain a clear impression of those that are lost.

Inscriptions form the sixth group of remains. With their help archaeologists are able to acquire a systematic understanding of thousands of years of history and culture. Often it is only these that make dumb monuments speak.

The study of such objects will always be the starting-point of archaeology, no matter how much actual methods may vary according to the notions of a particular period or the personal inclinations of individual scholars. But man-made objects are exposed to various kinds of deterioration, in particular to natural decay.

Man-made destruction, though, is no less formidable. At the time of Johann Joachim Winckelmann, the first and perhaps the most brilliant archaeologist, and for a few decades after his death in 1768, there were still valuable relics of antiquity to be found above ground. But these finds were soon exhausted, and they then had to be wrested from the earth into which they had sunk or which had drifted over them. Excavation, which at its outset was more like pillage, opened up entirely new perspectives to archaeology. For now archaeologists could see the remains in their original settings, part of their natural surroundings and the flow of history that brought them into being. In this way, what began rather as aesthetic contemplation became a world-wide science spanning the ages.

Below: Caravan of camels on the shore of the Aegean Sea, near the mouth of the River Cayster
Opposite: A view of the east side of Mount Olympus
Overleaf: Frieze on the marble sarcophagus of Alexander depicting a battle between Greeks and Persians. The figure on horseback represents Alexander the Great. Found at Sidon, it probably dates from about 310 BC (Istanbul Museum)

The Pyramids of Egypt

'Oh Egypt, Egypt – your religion will be a mere fable that your own children no longer believe . . .

'Nothing will remain but words carved in stone – painfully, men and gods will separate . . .

'And it will seem in vain that Egypt has worshipped the gods with devout hearts.'

Thus the priests prophesied in the last days of the Egyptian empire. The eternally-shifting sands drifted over the holy places. The relics that remained exposed stood silent.

And, with the triumph of Christianity at the end of the third century, knowledge of the 'sacred' hieroglyphic script was lost for 1,500 years. Egypt became a puzzle without a key, a playground for mystery-mongers and charlatans.

Opposite: The Great Pyramids at Giza
Below left: Bronze statuette of Isis with the Horus-child (Alexandria Museum)
Below right: Bronze statuette of Osiris (Alexandria Museum)

Not until Napoleon's expedition to Egypt in 1798, and the consequent opening up of the Nile valley, did events take a new course. During fortification works by French soldiers at Rosetta, a stone was discovered on which was carved a priestly decree in hieroglyphic, demotic and Greek language and characters. The Frenchman François Champollion was able to decipher the script and proceed in the following ten years to interpret all accessible inscriptions and papyri (1822).

When this scholar of genius died in 1832, the key was held to a real understanding of the history of Ancient Egypt. Only now was it possible to understand the Egyptian calendar, which was based on a division of the year into three seasons, and thereby distinguish the different periods in Egyptian history.

Left: Bust of François Champollion (Cairo Museum)
Below: Commemorative plaque in Arabic, French and English marking the discovery of the 'Rosetta Stone'. The plaque is fixed to a wall of the fort of St Julien at Rosetta, known today as Rashid, situated ten miles upstream from the mouth of the west branch of the Nile
Opposite: A 'pyramid text' or funerary text in hieroglyphic characters on the walls of the burial chamber in the pyramid of Unas at Saqqara, built in 2430 BC

Opposite: Terracotta figure (ten inches high) of a woman with raised arms and the head of a bird, a fertility symbol dating from about 4000 BC (British Museum, London)
Below: The Rosetta Stone, inscribed with a dedication by the priesthood of Heliopolis to Ptolemy V in 196 BC, written in hieroglyphic, demotic and Greek script. Its discovery in 1799 provided the key to hieroglyphic writing (British Museum, London)

1. *The prehistoric period, with the original African settlement along the Mediterranean coast and the poor nomadic tribes from the desert highlands of Arabia.*

2. *c. 2900–2700* BC
The period of the union between Lower and Upper Egypt under the sign of the god Horus, worshipped in both lands, and the reign of the Thinite kings (first and second dynasties), under whom the union of Upper and Lower Egypt was positively consolidated.

3. *c. 2700–2160* BC
The Old Kingdom, beginning with King Zoser, first ruler of the third dynasty; with the step pyramid at Saqqara, Zoser ushered in the age of the pyramids. The culminating period of the Old Kingdom (that which produced the Great Pyramids, later to become Wonders of the World, under Cheops, Chephren and Mycerinus), which ended with King Phiops, last ruler of the sixth dynasty, was followed by a period of decline (seventh–eleventh dynasties, 2540–2160 BC) leading to a bloody revolution which, however, paved the way to fresh development.

4. *2160–1785* BC
The 'Middle Kingdom', the age of the sun-god Re, in which the state became all-powerful.

5. *c. 1650* BC
The era of foreign rule by the Hyksos, the 'wicked', who forced their way in from the Near East and usurped the throne of the pharaohs for a hundred years; however, they brought the Egyptians the horse and war-chariot.

6. *1550–1085* BC
The 'New Empire' in which Egypt rose to world power (Amenophis I, 1525–1505 BC; Tuthmosis I, 1505–1483). It ended with Ramses III (twentieth dynasty) in 1085 BC.

7. *1085–332* BC
A long period of restoration which, though highly civilised, was also one of dissipation, in which Libyan mercenaries, Ethiopians, Assyrians and Persians held sway over Egypt.

8. *332–30* BC
The period of Macedonian rule under Alexander the Great and his successors, the clever and brilliant Ptolemies (Ptolemy I died 283 BC). The Ptolemaic kingdom ended with Cleopatra in the year 30 BC.

Landscape on the Nile delta near Rashid (Rosetta)

Below: Rock and desert around Dahshur, the most southerly site of the necropolises of the Old Kingdom
Opposite: Landscape on the Nile delta, with characteristic sailing barges

In ancient times, just as today, Egypt was a narrow strip of land, some 750 miles in length, stretching along both sides of the Nile, which rises in the swamps and mountain ranges of Central Africa. 175 miles from the Nile's outlet into the Mediterranean, this narrow strip of land broadens out to form a triangle with its apex pointing towards the south: the delta, so named by the Greeks after the similarly-shaped fourth letter of their alphabet.

At the time of the pharaohs, there were seven branches of the Nile flowing through the delta to the sea, gradually filling up with silt and soil. Today there are only two: the Rosetta branch on the west side and the Damietta on the east. To the east and west, the Nile valley is bordered by rocky desert slopes.

Here and there in these arid tracts are flourishing

oases where water seeps through from the Nile to feed springs and wells. The swaying of the palms in the wind seems like a *fata Morgana*.

The land under culture in ancient and modern Egypt totals only ten thousand square miles – in other words, it is less extensive than Belgium. The Nile and its associated canals, and the ideal climatic conditions, were and still remain the source of Egypt's wealth. The Egyptians tilled their vast Nile oasis with constant hard work and a high degree of skill, and very little has changed to this day.

To the Egyptians this living space seemed to have been specially carved out by their gods from the rest of the world: the perpetually green banks of the Nile, abundantly fertile, with three or more harvests a year pro-

viding all they needed to support them. The gleaming red and yellow desert on either side of the Nile valley was the world of the dead, the unknown, the foreigner. The mighty river marked out north and south for the Egyptians; upstream and downstream it provided the only through route across their kingdom, and held their villages, towns and provinces together like a clamp.

And above it all the sky, the infinite horizons, home of the gods and the secret powers that ruled over this land beside the Nile.

The city of On in Lower Egypt, which was called Heliopolis – the city of the sun – by the Greeks, plays a dominant role from the start. The god Atum, founder and lord of Heliopolis, becomes Atum-Re, king of the

gods. The symbol of his presence is the obelisk.

Horus, the god of light and justice, suspended above the heavens in the shape of a falcon with the sun and the moon for his eyes, becomes king of the world. He is lord of both Upper and Lower Egypt. Although separated politically, the northern and southern kingdoms are united in their worship of Horus.

In about 2900 BC King Narmer, ruler of the southern kingdom, united Lower and Upper Egypt politically as well. We can see this event and read about it on his victory tablet. Both sides are decorated at the top with cows' heads, symbols of the goddess Hathor, and between them is written the king's name. The obverse depicts in the centre two fabulous beasts being held on ropes by Egyptians; their necks are intertwined and

Left: Ammon-Re, the national god, and his wife, the earth-goddess Mut – a relief at the temple of Seti I at Abydos
Below: Cartouche of the Pharaoh Sesostris I, part of the relief on a pillar from Karnak (Cairo Museum)
Opposite: Victory palette of King Narmer (first dynasty) – obverse. Made of green slate, it dates from 3400 BC and comes from Hierakonpolis (Cairo Museum)

Below left: Detail from the reverse side of the victory palette of King Narmer (first dynasty) (Cairo Museum)
Below right: Tomb of King Menes, founder of the first dynasty, in the necropolis of Abydos
Bottom: Tomb of Osiris at Abydos – a view across the courtyard and the colonnaded entrance
Opposite: The war-goddess Sekhmet and the moon-god Thoth – fragment of a relief standing in front of the rear wall of the temple of Seti at Abydos

their heads are touching in a kiss – the northern and southern kingdoms united. Below this is the royal bull trampling down an enemy and at the same time breaking open a fortress with his horns. Above is a portrayal of the victory ceremony: here the king is wearing the crown of Lower Egypt which he has won in the battle. Four standards are being carried before him, two of them featuring the falcon of Horus. In front of these are the slain, laid out in rows with their severed heads between their legs. On the reverse side, the king stands in all his might, wearing the Upper Egyptian crown and striking down the enemy with his mace. Above is the falcon of Horus, holding a rope threaded through the upper lip of a head emerging from out of the ground. With the unification of the two kingdoms into one

state, Egypt's real historical existence begins. King Menes is the first of the long line of pharaohs. In him, and in all the pharaohs, the god Horus is made incarnate: the king becomes god. In Abydos, near one of the royal residences, he built a necropolis containing the royal tombs of the earliest dynasties and the sacred tomb of Osiris.

King Menes, founder of the first dynasty, is presumed to have been buried in the Abydos necropolis. The tomb ascribed to him is one of the oldest known brick buildings in the world.

Kha'sekhemui, the last king of the second dynasty, built himself a stone chamber in Abydos surrounded by corridors containing brick niches for his court officials. The king is the 'king of the two lands', the incarnation of Horus, suckled by the lion-headed war goddess Sekhmet from Memphis, and himself a lion or a lion with a human head, striking down the nations with his claws. What was written of the goddess Sekhmet applies also to him:

'Her countenance shone like the sun, her eyes glowed with fire, the desert was veiled in dust when she struck the ground with her tail.'

The king, like the gods, is lord of life and death, whom subjects approach in fear and trembling to kiss the dust at his feet. Yet he is bound by ceremonials such as the gods demand. At the feast of the king's reconsecration, celebrated every thirty years, the king ascends separate flights of steps to two thrones: in the white crown of Upper Egypt, and in the red crown of Lower Egypt.

Below left: King Semerset I (twelfth dynasty), in the guise of Osiris, wearing the crown of Upper Egypt – a gigantic statue from the temple of Ammon at Karnak (Cairo Museum)
Below right: King Mentuhotep, wearing the crown of Lower Egypt, dressed for the Heb-Sed festival – statue of painted sandstone (Cairo Museum)

Below left: Ivory statuette of King Cheops (fourth dynasty), seated. He was the builder of the oldest and biggest of the three pyramids at Giza (Cairo Museum)

Below right: Alabaster statuette of King Chephren (fourth dynasty), seated. He built the second largest pyramid at Giza (Cairo Museum)

The king must celebrate the birthdays of Min, the god of fertility, who ensures and guards the nation's harvests; Anubis of Siut with the dog's head, god of the dead, 'master of the mortuary' and 'lord of the cemetery'; Bastet of Bubastis with the cat's head, goddess of joy; and the god Apis, the sacred bull of Memphis.

With his accession to the throne, the king, 'the great god', chooses his temporal and his eternal dwelling-place. He knows that in the life to come he has to answer for his deeds 'before the great god, the lord of judgment', and that only a just and devout life can secure him a happy afterlife.

King Zoser, with whom the third dynasty came to power, found a physical symbol to represent the everlasting power of the king: on the desert plateau near

Saqqara, close to his capital at Memphis, he had his own necropolis built.

Thus prayed the priests:
'The gates of heaven will be opened to you, the gates of the cooling water will be unlocked to you . . .'.

The originator and architect of the necropolis was Imhotep, the king's first minister, later deified for his wisdom in the realms of architecture and medicine. Imhotep assembled in one place the tombs of the Upper and Lower Egyptian kings, and associated them in people's minds with Zoser's earthly residence in Memphis.

The thirty-two-foot-high boundary wall with its fourteen imitation doorways and one entrance gate constitutes the 'White Wall', the chief characteristic of

Memphian building. It forms a regular rectangle measuring three hundred yards by six hundred yards. A path leads through a colonnade into the main courtyard, on the left of which is the south tomb, a ninety-foot-deep shaft. At this symbolic meeting-point of north and south are buried the king's entrails. Here too resides Ka, the spirit, the spiritual force of the ruler.

From the main courtyard the path continues through a little temple to the Heb-Sed courtyard, which was presumably designed to allow the king to go on attending the great festival of his jubilee even after death – again, a symbol of the king's everlasting power.

Passing the 'House of the North' and the 'House of the South', symbolising Lower and Upper Egypt, the path leads on to a completely enclosed stone chamber.

This contained and concealed the image of the king. Two peep-holes provided his contact with the outside world.

Adjoining its right-hand corner, against the front of the pyramid, stood the mortuary chapel, whence led the only way through into the tomb chamber.

Even if Imhotep still failed to find the perfect outward form to express the concept and cultural significance of Zoser, his king, he nonetheless created something more for the divine kingship than an architectural stage-set. Had he not had any successors, we should certainly know of no other and better way for a building to symbolise the concept of 'on Earth as it is in Heaven'.

The well-ordered state, the close-knit ordering of society, have their continuation in the afterlife. And the

influence of the divine has its earthly representation in the life of the king. As long as they are both in harmony, earthly order is not endangered and the gods are not threatened.

King Snefru, with whom the fourth dynasty began, waged war against the Nubians and led seven thousand men and women to Egypt as captives. He brought forty shiploads of costly cedarwood from the Lebanon, and fought successfully against the Bedouins. At Medum, in the northern province of Upper Egypt, he built a step pyramid for his predecessor Huni that was probably intended to be covered over with a sloping casing, but remained unfinished, and at Dahshur he built another which was the first true pyramid in shape. He was also responsible for the great stone pyramid at Dahshur, built at an earlier date, the so-called 'Bent Pyramid'; its shape is a transitional stage between the step pyramid and the true pyramid. His building-programme was so vast that he monopolised the labour force of the entire kingdom during his twenty-four-year reign. The stones, quarried throughout the year by skilled stone-masons – whenever agricultural work came to a complete halt during the inundation – were loaded, transported across the river and hauled up enormous ramps to the heights of the desert plateaux by peasants from the whole of Egypt working under compulsory labour.

The focal point of the kingdom was now Memphis, lying on the Nile at the very boundary between Upper and Lower Egypt. Here stood the temple of Ptah, creator of all things and sole author of the divine word.

Opposite: Wooden wall panel depicting Hesire, an official of the third dynasty, carrying sceptre, staff and writing implement; from his tomb at Saqqara (Cairo Museum)
Below: General view of the pyramid complex at Dahshur, seen from the top of the entrance-gate to Zoser's pyramid at Saqqara
Bottom left: The North Pyramid of Snefru at Dahshur
Bottom right: Egyptians towing a sailing barge through a lock on the Nile
Overleaf: A column of Nubian police on the march – figures of painted wood from the tomb of a twelfth-dynasty prince of Asyut (Cairo Museum)

What is known as the Memphitic Theology says of him: 'He created the gods, he made the cities, he set up the gods in their holy places and made their bodies as they wanted them.' The will of the king was all-powerful.

His chief spokesman was the 'Vizier and Judge of the Great Porch', usually a prince of the reigning household. He headed the king's chancellery, and one of his main duties was administering the nation's finances.

'Law and order' was maintained by Nubian soldiers and police armed with bows and arrows. In time of war, peasant contingents were enlisted in the provinces.

The numerous officials trained at the offices in the temple all bore the title of 'scribes'. They worked in the administrative departments known as 'houses', e.g., the house of food, the house of weapons, the house of

Opposite: Colossal statue of the god Ptah (Cairo Museum)
Below: Remains of the walls and columns of the temple of Ptah at Memphis

Below: Painted limestone statue of a scribe (fourth dynasty) found at Saqqara; the eyes are outlined in copper, the eyeballs are made of bone and the irises of polished crystal against a background of ebony (Cairo Museum)

fields. Everything was organised and controlled down to the minutest detail.

One office in particular was that of 'superintendent of workers and craftsmen', whose task it was to recruit the armies of workers and supervise their activities. They and their work were of vital importance to the pharaohs and their life-long planning and building.

The provinces were ruled by regional governors, the 'monarchs'. They dispensed law and collected the taxes. Under them were the village magistrates, who were responsible for law and order, tax-returns, and the prompt and accurate settling of accounts in their particular villages. Censuses and surveys were eagerly undertaken. The inspector of royal property supervised the king's revenue, which consisted of produce from his

estates and taxes in the form of tribute in kind and compulsory labour from his subjects. Symbol of the royal prerogative, the measuring-rod used on the king's behalf was one-sixth longer than for ordinary mortals.

The bulk of the peasantry was tied to the soil. They worked on the estates of the king and others of high rank who were entitled to compulsory labour from the peasants. The work was carefully reckoned by the hour.

Although gold and silver did serve as measures of value, and determined prices and rates of pay, generally a system of trading in kind operated throughout Egypt. The people and the officials lived 'from the king's table'. The temples were built only at the king's command and, like the one at Abydos, faced the Nile, the bestower of life.

Below left: Painted limestone statue of an unknown officer (Cairo Museum)
Below right: Ka-Aper, a village magistrate – wooden statue from Saqqara, about 2600 BC (Cairo Museum)
Bottom: Gathering the taxes, a model in painted wood from an eleventh-dynasty tomb (Cairo Museum)

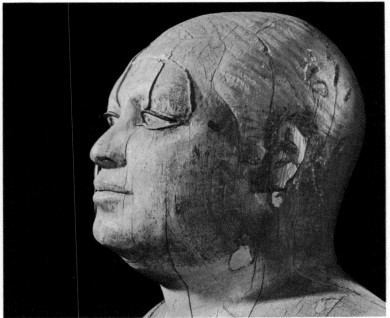

From the landing-place where his boat is moored, the king strides up the processional way to the first forecourt, the one that is open to the people. He is accompanied by the princes and princesses of his household. The king proceeds through the second forecourt, reserved for his presence alone, to the portico adorned with pictures of kings and gods.

And then he enters the shrine itself, the hall of the thirty-six columns and seven holy chapels. Here in the half-light of the sacred mysteries, the god-king lingers in communion with the gods, as mediator between heaven and earth, benefactor and judge of his people.

Permanently-appointed priests, including teachers, officiated in the temples. Over them, princes of the royal household were appointed as high priests. In this way

Below: Entrance to the courtyard of the temple of Seti at Abydos
Opposite: A view through the entrance to the temple of Seti at Abydos

Below: Women grinding corn, from a sixth-dynasty tomb, about 2400 BC (Cairo Museum)
Opposite left: The high priest Ka-em-Ked – painted limestone figure with inlaid eyes, fourth or fifth dynasty, found at Saqqara (Cairo Museum)
Opposite right: King Mycerinus (fourth dynasty) with two goddesses – a slate sculpture (seen here from the side) from the mortuary chapel of Mycerinus's pyramid at Giza (Cairo Museum)

the lands belonging to the temple hierarchy, for the most part extensive, remained under royal control. For all the king's absolute authority as a god on earth associating with gods and goddesses, deciding each and every action in society, and punishing every violation of this divine order, there was nonetheless a kind of patriarchal benevolence or devout humanitarianism spreading downwards through the community. Men lived their petty lives, which, despite work and hardship, constituted their whole happiness. The women worked and dreamed of love and happiness. The mothers bore children. The children ran about and exercised. The girls played and danced, and not just when rituals provided the occasion. Petty thefts and such minor sensations provided the evening's gossip.

Right: Man fishing from a boat with a line – a relief in the tomb of Ti at Saqqara, fifth dynasty

Below: Man with herons – a relief in the tomb of Ptahhotep at Saqqara, fifth dynasty

The men bred dogs and monkeys and took them out hunting. They fished the Nile with rods or nets, and their eyes, despite sweat and tears, remained open to the beauties of this world.

King Cheops, an energetic ruler of the early fourth dynasty, produced with his pyramid the mightiest building the world has ever known.

The square base measures 755 feet on each side. The pyramid, built on the rocky ledge projecting from the limestone plateau, was originally over 480 feet high. The inner mass of the pyramid consists of rough-hewn and irregularly laid limestone blocks, while the outer casing is of well-cut and neatly joined blocks. Most of this casing has now come away, having been used for building material.

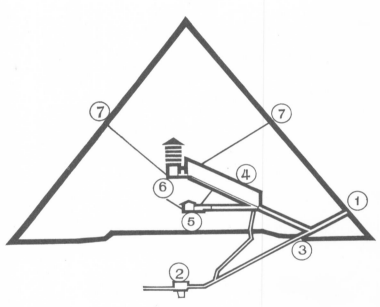

Opposite left: The gallery leading up through the interior of Cheops's pyramid to the burial chamber known as the King's Chamber. The gallery is 138 feet long and twenty-eight feet high
Opposite below: Cross-section through the pyramid of Cheops at Giza: 1 original entrance, 2 subterranean burial chamber, 3 passage to subterranean chamber, 4 grand gallery, 5 small burial chamber, the so-called Queen's Chamber, 6 large burial chamber, the so-called King's Chamber, 7 ventilation shafts
Opposite bottom: Original entrance to Cheops's pyramid, now no longer usable
Below: The pyramid of Cheops at Giza and, in the foreground, the mortuary chapel of Chephren's pyramid

The original entrance to the pyramid is on the north side at a height of sixty feet. From here there is a 320-foot-long passage leading down through the living rock at a slope of twenty-seven degrees to an underground burial chamber. It was aligned with the Pole Star, the reigning prince of the firmament.

The pharaoh, the 'Pole Star of the earth', thereby illustrated his hope and desire to ascend from earth to heaven and overcome human mortality. A second passage, 125 feet long with a very low ceiling, slopes upwards from ground level within the pyramid. It then takes a horizontal course and increases in height, enabling one to walk upright. This passage ends in a chamber situated directly beneath the tip of the pyramid and sixty-five feet above ground level. It is so regularly

lined with Tura limestone that it appears to be cut straight out of the rock. An extension of the passage comes to an abrupt end, and the unfinished floor of the chamber may be taken to indicate that the project was finally abandoned.

The builders then went back to the original upward-sloping passage. They extended it upwards by another 138 feet, though this time as a large gallery of over six feet in width and more than twenty-seven feet high. The gallery is lined with Moqattam limestone. It leads through a small ante-room and opens out into the burial chamber itself, which is lined with black granite and once again lies almost directly below the tip of the pyramid.

The granite sarcophagus of the pharaoh was found

Below: The 'king list' in the temple of Seti I at Abydos contains the names of all the kings from Menes, founder of the first dynasty, down to Seti I of the nineteenth dynasty

Far right: The east wall of the uncompleted original burial chamber for King Cheops in his pyramid at Giza (known erroneously as the 'Queen's Chamber')

The granite sarcophagus of King Cheops in the Great Pyramid at Giza, located in the upper chamber, the burial chamber proper. On its discovery the cover was found to be broken open and the coffin empty

to be empty on its discovery, and the cover missing. In order to prevent grave-robbers from gaining access to the pyramid, closing up the entrance and the passageways was one of the most important tasks that confronted the builders. Massive stone barriers were arranged in such a way that they could be let down after the funeral ceremony. In spite of these, it is likely that the pharaoh had already been snatched from his grave by revolutionaries at the end of the Old Kingdom.

Cheops's pyramid, called 'Horizon of Cheops', could easily contain St Peter's in Rome, the cathedrals of Milan and Florence, St Paul's Cathedral and Westminster Abbey in London – in other words, the five biggest churches in the world. It is the largest building of all time, including the present day.

Re-Dedef, Cheops's successor – he reigned only eight years – had his monument built further to the north. His pyramid, begun at Abu-Roash and facing Heliopolis, the city of the sun-god, was never completed. Re-Dedef, one of the sons of Cheops who fought bitterly amongst themselves, served only to bridge over the dynasty until his brother Chephren came to the throne. That he was the fourth dynasty's legitimate successor follows from the fact that he reverted to Giza for the siting of his tomb. To the south-west of Cheops's Great Pyramid, Chephren had his own pyramid built on the same rocky plateau. It was called 'Great is Chephren' and is constructed on the same principles as Cheops's pyramid.

Mycerinus, Chephren's son and successor, built the

Re-Dedef, the successor of King Cheops (fourth dynasty) – a fragment (Cairo Museum)

third pyramid, called 'God-like is Mycerinus', on the extreme south-west of the Giza plateau. It is the smallest of the pyramids, and, together with the two large ones and the Sphinx placed further towards the east, towards the sunrise, forms one of the 'Seven Wonders of the World'.

The pyramids themselves, considered on their own, are wonders of the man-made world. But they are only a part of the burial complex. The total area included the portico or valley temple situated on the banks of the Nile, the causeway leading up to the desert plateau, over two miles long, the mortuary chapel at the foot of each pyramid with its forecourt and colonnade, and the pyramid towering up behind.

The whole state is concentrated in the person of the

Below: Cylinder seal of King Chephren, made of stone (right), and an impression from it; it reads 'Beloved of Hathor' – in other words, beloved of the gods. The seal dates from about 2650 BC
Bottom: Uncompleted pyramid of King Re-Dedef at Abu-Roash
Opposite: The pyramid of Chephren at Giza with, in the foreground, the causeway leading from the valley temple to the mortuary chapel

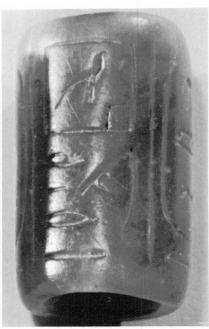

pharaoh, the great god. The highest duty of the state is to maintain the king's sovereignty even after death, and for all eternity. His entrails are preserved against corruption in jars which have heads of the sons of Horus for covers; his body is preserved for all time by embalming. His heart is replaced by a stone scarab, emblem of the sun-god, on which are carved the words: 'O heart, do not bear witness against me'. The person thus immortalised is protected against violence and destruction from outside by the building in which he is housed. An ample supply of food is left for the dead person – or the living person, as he is in fact regarded. Vessels, stands and tables with recesses for the fluids and ointments are laid out for making religious offerings. A likeness of the deceased is set up for the dead man's spirit to enter.

Below: King Chephren wearing a head-cloth and backed by the falcon of Horus – detail from the seated figure in dark-green diorite found in the mortuary chapel of his pyramid at Giza (Cairo Museum)
Opposite: King Mycerinus with goddesses (Cairo Museum)

Below: Boat with a mummy beneath a canopy – painted wooden model from a tomb (British Museum, London)
Bottom: Jars used for storing the entrails of the dead when their bodies were embalmed; they were placed under the protection of individual deities, featured on the lids (Pelizäus Museum, Hildesheim, West Germany)
Opposite: False door from the tomb of Ateti at Saqqara, through which the Ka, or spirit, of the dead man could pass (Cairo Museum)

A large stone tablet in the shape of a closed door, the so-called 'false door', is incorporated in the tomb; this is the entrance to the spirit world. The world that surrounded the living person is supposed to remain about him in death: family, servants, fields and cattle, birds and fishes, farmhands and oxen, and all the good things of this life. To prolong man's brief life for all eternity, and make possible the seemingly impossible – that is what the cult of the dead aims to achieve.

And the pharaoh, the great god, has his family participate in his immortality: wives and children, members of his household, and the highest officials in the land.

Around the tombs of the pharaohs are necropolises for members of the royal family. Row after row of tombs are laid out in regular avenues. What was built for the

Below left: Statue of Ti, a high-ranking court dignitary towards the end of the fifth dynasty; his is the largest and most beautiful of the tombs at Saqqara (Cairo Museum)
Below right: The wife of a high-ranking officer of the nineteenth dynasty – crystalline limestone (Cairo Museum)
Opposite: Egyptian dignitary with wife and son – limestone, 2400 BC

98

king on a vast and superhuman scale is here repeated in easily comprehensible proportions.

The slaves, peasants and workers lie huddled together in their graves, with no inscriptions or sculptures, and take no part in the life to come.

But the ground began to shake beneath the living pharaohs, though Egypt was now the centre of the world.

Pharaohs still occupied the throne, but the priests of Heliopolis grew more and more powerful. The sun-god Re became the new god on earth, and the kings became his servants. Behind the royal city of Memphis arose the sun-temple of Abusir. The concept of the divine kingship faded away. Re became the national god and ruler of the world, and the king his obedient son who carried out his wishes.

The last ruler of the sixth dynasty, Merenre II, was assassinated. The provincial princes rose up against the king, divided up the kingdom and seized the power for themselves. The hungry population rose up in rebellion.

A papyrus of the time gives us this description: 'The country has spun like a potter's wheel. Slaves and paupers have plundered the homes of the aristocrats. Former gentlemen and ladies are performing the meanest slave-work. Families are destroying each other because of their hunger. The government offices have been plundered, the documents torn to pieces. The tombs have been opened and the royal mummies snatched from their coffins. To those who have lived through this it is as if the Nile were flowing with blood, and new-born infants are already longing to leave this world.'

The pharaohs of the Old Kingdom, which stood for a thousand years, are now dethroned. The pyramids of Giza, the first and the oldest of the Seven Wonders of the Ancient World, remain to bear witness to their power and their greatness.

The sphinx and the pyramids at Giza – the first and by far the
oldest of the Seven Wonders of the World

The Hanging Gardens of Semiramis

Below: The outer and inner walls of Babylon with the Euphrates river in the foreground – a model of the city as it was at the time of Nebuchadnezzar II (Babylon Museum)
Far right: Female idol of clay (five inches high), Sumerian, found at Mari and dating from about 2000 BC (Aleppo Museum)

Thus spoke Ishtar, Babylon's great goddess of love and death, to the king: 'I will protect you as a mother protects her children, I will shelter you between my breasts like a jewel on my necklace.' And the king told his city: 'I love you, Babylon, as I love my own precious life! May all the kings of the world and all mankind pay you their tribute. May you endure for all eternity.'

Babylon, 'the heavenly city', with its two highways, three canals, eight city gates and twenty-four streets, with its fifty-three temples to the great gods and hundreds of chapels to Ishtar and the seven spirits of heaven and the seven gods of the earth, was dominated by the temple of Marduk, the most powerful of all the gods. The king's palaces and the Hanging Gardens of Queen Semiramis were renowned, and the latter were

reckoned among the Seven Wonders of the Ancient World.

Isaiah, too, the prophet of Israel, praised Babylon as 'the glory of the kingdoms, the beauty of the Chaldees' excellency'. But he prophesied the fall of the city as in 'Sodom and Gomorrah; it shall never be inhabited, neither shall it be dwelt in . . . but owls shall dwell there . . . and the wild beasts shall cry in their desolate houses.' His words came true: the walls of Babylon fell; Ashur, the mighty city in the north, the terror of the peoples, was laid low; also Ur in the south, the city of the giant temples and the great gods.

Mesopotamia – land between the rivers – was the name given by the Greek historian Polybius in the second century BC to the region enclosed by the Tigris

and the Euphrates: to the south, the land of Sumer with the cities of Ur, Uruk and Babylon, later to be known as the kingdom of Babylonia; and to the north, Assyria, with the cities of Ashur, Dur-Sharrukin and Nineveh. The word Mesopotamia was also used by the translators of the Old Testament in Alexandria to render the reference in Genesis to *Aram-naharaim* – Aram of the rivers, the home of Abraham. Thus, with the various translations of the Bible, the word Mesopotamia became known throughout the whole of Europe. Today we define Mesopotamia as the land between the mountains of Kurdistan in the north and the swamps of the river delta on the Persian Gulf in the south, and between the plains and deserts of Jordan and Syria in the east and the mountain ranges of Iran in the west.

Within this rectangle many civilisations flourished in the course of four thousand years, beginning at the close of the Stone Age and ending abruptly with the fall of Babylon in the year 539 BC.

The climate has scarcely altered since the days when the mountain-dwellers moved down to the river plains in the fifth millennium BC. But the soil has altered owing to the silting up of the rivers and because of the rock-debris they carry with them. The sea-coast has also been pushed outwards for the same reasons.

But, just as today the nomads ride through the deserts and grassland with their herds to find the best pastures for their livestock, regardless of frontiers and political divisions, so the hosts of Assyrians and Babylonians drove westwards to the sea. Their aim was to control

Opposite below: Water-buffalo, after the donkey the most common of the larger domestic animals in Mesopotamia
Opposite bottom: The reed-covered banks of the Tigris near Ashur, today known as Al Aqr
Right: Prehistoric female idol of clay, found at Tell Sawan (Iraq Museum, Baghdad)
Below: Painted clay dish (12·8 inches in diameter) of the so-called Halafian culture in the first half of the fifth century BC, found at Arpatshiya (Iraq Museum, Baghdad)

Below: Four-horse chariot of bronze, Me-silim period, fourth or third century BC (Iraq Museum, Baghdad)
Opposite: The sheer rock near Behistun (also called Bisitun) which bears the famous inscription of Darius; its trilingual text led to the deciphering of cuneiform script

the caravan trails along the Mediterranean coast to the 'land flowing with milk and honey' and draw profit from them.

Our knowledge of the history of this mysterious land of Mesopotamia was acquired comparatively recently. In the year 1625 the Italian nobleman Pietro della Valle made a journey through Mesopotamia, taking in Ur and Babylon, and brought back to Europe the first examples of the mysterious cuneiform script. No one was able to read them.

In 1790 the *Journal des Savants* published reports by the Abbé de Beauchamp concerning the famous Tower of Babel and its ruins. Whereupon the East India Company in London asked their agent Claudius James Rich to send bricks bearing the inscriptions to England. The

samples that arrived in London caused considerable astonishment, but they could not be deciphered.

Finally, in 1842, the English officer Henry Rawlinson discovered at Behistun, on the route from Hamadan to Kermanshah near the western border of Iran, a relief cut 160 feet up in the precipitous rock and dating from the year 500 BC. It was a victory monument set up by Darius I, the Persian king of the dynasty of the Achaemenids, and on it are carved the names of the inhabitants of vanquished nations who paid homage to the king of kings. Beneath this Darius gives details of his battles and victories in Old Persian, Elamite and Babylonian written in cuneiform script. In extremely difficult conditions Rawlinson copied out thousands of characters in his own hand, hoping that by comparing the written words with the spoken language he could make sense of the unintelligible script of the Babylonians. But it was not until six years later that scholars were able to translate the Elamite text with its 111 symbols.

But they still failed to unravel the Babylonian cuneiform script. Five hundred different combinations of cuneiform characters were discovered, but no alphabet. Not until the discovery by the Irishman Hincks that a character could stand for a syllable as well as a whole word was a breakthrough achieved.

Excavations began in 1842 near Mosul, conducted by the French consul Paul Emile Botta, who dug mainly at Dur-Sharrukin (the present-day Khorsabad), the seat and temple-city of King Sargon II of Assyria, and thus uncovered the famous Assyrian sculptures of the eighth

century BC, which the world greeted with admiration and amazement.

The Englishman Austen Henry Layard, who began operations in 1845, was the second great pioneer of excavation in Mesopotamia. He dug mainly in Nimrud, south of Nineveh on the Tigris and capital of Assyria since the reign of Ashurnasirpal I. The resulting discovery of the *lamassus*, gigantic winged figures, half man, half lion, that stood guard at the gates, created a worldwide sensation.

Around 1850 the English archaeologist Sir Henry Rawlinson uncovered more of King Ashurbanipal's palace in Nineveh, and found a vast royal library of clay tablets with invaluable documents on Babylonian history and literature.

Below: Remains of the north gate of the palace of Sargon II at Dur-Sharrukin (the present-day Khorsabad)
Bottom: Bust of Sir Austen Henry Layard (1817–94), the noted British archaeologist (British Museum, London)
Opposite: A *lamassu*, or winged lion with human head, which stood guard at the gate of King Ashurnasirpal's palace at Nineveh – New Assyrian period (British Museum, London)

Researches were now extended to the religious centres of the Sumerian nation in the southern part of the Land of the Two Rivers, in particular to the towns of Ur and Uruk, Nippur and Eridu, for thousands of years the most important royal residences and centres of worship in southern Babylonia.

Not until the turn of the century did methodical exploration and opening up of whole city districts and temple complexes begin. The German scholars Robert Koldewey in Babylon and Uruk and Walter Andrae in Ashur made outstanding contributions at this time.

There are still undiscovered treasures lying here in the earth, and many problems waiting to be solved. The skull of a cave-dweller found in the Shanidar valley in northern Mesopotamia is estimated by scientists to be

sixty thousand years old. The foundations of the oldest village in Mesopotamia were found at Jarmo, near the present-day village of Shemshemal in the north-east of the region. Bowls, containers and female terra-cotta figures indicate considerable manual skill on the part of these people and a distinct feeling for shape and colour. They reveal an aptitude for the grand gesture, for things sacred and monumental.

We cannot precisely locate the cradle of the civilisation of the Sumerians, the inhabitants of the land of Sumer between the Tigris and the Euphrates that extended roughly from present-day Baghdad to the Persian Gulf. But many believe that Sumer means the begetter, the male sexual organ, the deed. Primitive myths that had stirred men's minds for thousands of

years were fixed by the Sumerians in solid and visible images, to save them from being forgotten. In places such as Uruk they built the heavenly citadels, the ziggurats, the high-towering, the meeting-place of men and gods. For Anu, the heaven, they built the 'white temple' in Uruk, as if they wished to provide an earthly reflection of the mighty power which encompassed and dominated the world.

On the Ziggurat of Eanna they built the temple of Ishtar, goddess of sensual love, without whose blessing all procreation ceased. At the same time, as war goddess, she was mistress over death.

As the sacramental vases of Uruk indicate, the people of Sumer sacrificed the produce of their fields and the young of their herds to the two-faced goddess of

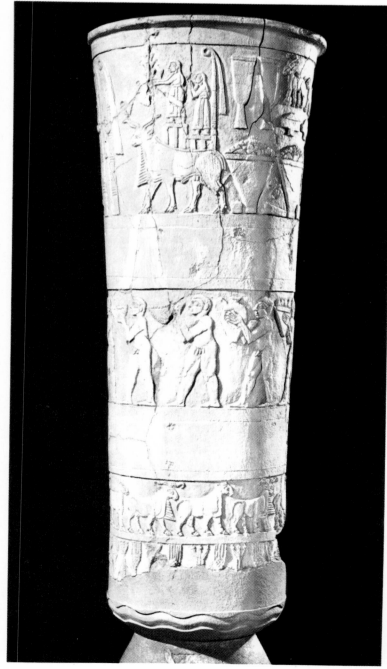

Left: Gilgamesh clasping a lion – relief from Dur-Sharrukin (Louvre, Paris)

Below: Alabaster female head (8.5 inches high) dating from the end of the fourth millennium BC and found at Warka (ancient Uruk); the eyes and eyebrows were originally inlaid (Iraq Museum, Baghdad)

Opposite: Victory stele of Eannatum of Lagash, known as the 'stele of the vultures' – about 2800 BC (Louvre, Paris)

life and death, sensual pleasure and bitter revenge, these sacrifices themselves being suspended between war and peace, life and death.

Sumer's mythical hero was Gilgamesh, the legendary king of Uruk, two-thirds god and one-third man, 'he who saw everything, all the way to the end of the earth' and 'unveiled what was hidden'. This bold hero won Enkidu the Mighty of the mountains and plains as a friend, then lost him through death. Though Gilgamesh sought to overcome the fear of death, he had to recognise that victory over death was impossible. His one consolation was that Uruk and Uruk's walls were firm and everlasting.

The alabaster female head found in the Eanna temple is one of the first clues to the history of the Sumerian nation. The era of human dominance begins. The early dynastic period commences in about the year 2800 BC.

Men started to quarrel, kill and conquer in the name of the gods, as is shown on the stele of the 'gods' viceroy', Eannatum of Lagash; he is seen overcoming the enemy, heaping up their corpses in great mounds, and celebrating his victory on the mountain of dead. The vultures in the sky are flying before the king and his victorious army with scraps from the slaughtered enemy corpses and carrying them as a mark of triumph to the god who is aiding the king in the battle. In one hand he holds an enormous net filled with the enemies of Lagash whom he has captured. And he is killing them one after the other with his enormous club.

Kings succeeded kings, power and glory passed from

Left: Seated figure of the scribe Dudu, from the third millennium BC (Iraq Museum, Baghdad)

Opposite left: Lifesize bronze head of an Akkadian prince, presumed to be Sargon I – from Nineveh, about 2600 BC (Iraq Museum, Baghdad)

Opposite right: Royal tomb at Ur, built in about 2250 BC; the vault is thirty-six feet long and twenty-six feet high

Bottom: Frieze from a temple at Ur – Sumerian, predynastic period (Iraq Museum, Baghdad)

Ur to Lagash, to Kish, to Akkad, but it was still the same ancient country of Sumer.

The scribes administered the country for the kings. They calculated the taxes, which led to the wise saying: 'You may have a master, you may have a king, but the man you should really fear is the tax-collector'. The result of such wisdom was that every now and again the people overthrew their kings – but not the scribes – and put new ones in their place.

When Sargon of Akkad (2414–2358 BC) – a country lying to the north of Sumer – attacked and destroyed Uruk, razed the walls of Ur, conquered Lagash and established Semitic rule throughout southern Mesopotamia, a new phase began in this country's history which lasted just two hundred years.

The armies of Naramsin, a successor to Sargon, marched as far as the shores of the Mediterranean and the Black Sea. They spilt the blood of innocent peoples, but they enabled nations and tribes from Syria to Transcaucasia and on into Persia to build up their own power on the already highly-developed Sumerian civilisation which the invaders established.

When the Guti, a barbarian tribe from the highlands of eastern Mesopotamia, put out the eyes of the statue of Sargon, cut off its ears and docked its beard, this was the symbol of the hundred-year subjugation of the kingdom of Sumer and Akkad, the destruction of its cities and the burning down of its temples.

But when Ur-nammu, the first king of the third dynasty of Ur, assumed power, the name of the Guti

was obliterated, the kingdom of Sumer and Akkad re-united, and Ur-nammu could proudly proclaim himself 'King of the four corners of the earth'. The Ziggurat, the 'high-towering', stood once again in Ur, with a temple of blue-glazed bricks on its highest terrace.

Shulgi, Ur-nammu's son, built the royal tombs of Ur to protect the bodies and souls of his ancestors. For the power of the king was divine, rule and religion were inseparable, and the fate of the kings was also the fate of their people. Ibi-sin, the last king of the magnificent third dynasty of Ur, was taken prisoner by his enemies.

Control of Mesopotamia went for a time to the lords of Mari, the powerful city on the Euphrates. The life-giving goddess of Mari became a symbol of the continuing existence of the kingdoms, although it was

co-existence among city-states and their gods that for two centuries determined the course of their history.

In the same way, at an earlier date, the 'gods' viceroys' of Lagash, the city on the Tigris, had strongly influenced the development of Sumer: they set up their images in the temples and had sacrifices made to them.

Hammurabi, a member of the nomadic Amorite tribe, came to the throne of Babylon in 1793 BC, united the divided country and centralised control in his own hands. Larsa, the ambitious city to the south of Uruk, was conquered by him. Mari, the proud city across the Euphrates which had tried to dominate the rest of Sumer, was also taken and destroyed. The ancient kingdom of Eshnunna, to the north-east of present-day Baghdad, was ruthlessly subjugated. And there was even a Babylonian garrison in Qalat Sherqat, the capital of Assyria. The victorious Monarch of Ishtar-Inanna, the great goddess of Uruk and Ur, built a temple at Ishchali, on ancient Babylonian territory: reconciliation with the tradition of Sumer. Events had turned full circle.

Hammurabi set up the many-faced god in the temples, the one who 'called the four corners of the earth to obedience'. He now reigned from the Taurus mountains in the north to the Persian Gulf in the south, and his officials controlled the towns, villages and caravan routes. The kingdom was united, above all by the Code of Hammurabi, which in its 282 paragraphs embraced the whole of human life: litigation, property and estate, money dealings, family law, rents, slaves, temple

service, house and shipbuilding, physical injury, adoption – nothing was omitted.

As the lord of Babylon proclaimed: 'insomuch as Marduk sent me to lead the people and restore the nation, I have established law and justice in the land and fostered the well-being of my subjects'.

Nevertheless Hammurabi's death (1750 BC) was the signal for uprisings throughout the country.

And into Babylon came the priest-kings of the Hittites, a warrior nation from the mountains of Asia Minor. After exactly three hundred years, the Babylonian kingdom had ceased to exist.

The Cissians, also known as the Kassites, from the north-east of Persia, brought this desolate interlude to a close. They came down from their mountains into the

Below: Lion from the side of a doorway in the temple of Ninurta at Kalakh, at the time of Ashurnasirpal II, about 880 BC – New Assyrian period (British Museum, London)

Bottom: War-chariot – detail from a relief showing a battle-scene, from the royal palace at Kalakh (now Nimrud) (Iraq Museum, Baghdad)

Opposite left: Boundary-stone from the time of Nebuchadnezzar I, king of Babylon; the markings define the rights of a high-ranking official – about 1140 BC (British Museum, London)

Opposite right: Colossal statue of Shalmaneser III, king of Ashur (Istanbul Museum)

plains of the Tigris and the Euphrates and ruled there for over four hundred years. Their god was Marduk, the lord of Babylon. In about 1340 BC the Kassites built their own capital at Dur-Kurigalzu. They carried on a brisk exchange-trade with Egypt, the land on the Nile. And the pharaoh, still a powerful ruler, whom the Kassite king called 'brother', was approached with a request to send one of his daughters to Dur-Kurigalzu to be the king's bride. 'There are enough grown-up daughters,' wrote the Kassite king to the pharaoh with artful good humour as the latter hesitated; 'send any beautiful woman you choose – who will say that she is not a king's daughter?'

Only Ashur resisted the Kassites. When the Assyrian armies began to march, Kassite rule came to an end.

King Tukulti-Ninurta (1245–1208 BC) subjugated the southern part of Mesopotamia, deported twenty-eight thousand men from Syria and brought the god Marduk from Babylon to Ashur as a victory trophy.

But when the king was assassinated by his own son in the course of an uprising, Ashur temporarily lost the control and leadership of Mesopotamia.

Nebuchadnezzar I, the king of Babylon (1128–1106 BC), pacified the northern mountain-dwellers who were constantly attempting to invade the south. He defeated the Elamites from the highlands of south-west Persia, and transferred control of Mesopotamia from Ashur to Babylon. But only thirty years later the land of Ashur, under its god Ashur, had freed itself once more from all bondage.

In Ashur King Tiglath-pileser I (1116–1077 BC) built the twin temple to Anu, the Sumerian god of the heavens, and Adad, the Babylonian god of the thunderstorm. He had the Ziggurat built up high as a symbol of the united kingdom over which he ruled. Ashur's troops thrust forward to the shores of the Mediterranean.

Under Ashurnasirpal II (883–859 BC), the kingdom extended from the River Khabur to the Zagros mountains in western Iran, and from Nisibis in the north to Samawa in the south.

In Kalakh, today called Nimrud, Ashurnasirpal built his palace; it covered five acres. Size, labour, expense – nothing was spared. He invited 69,574 guests from all parts of the kingdom. A relief at the base of the throne in Kalakh shows what the king ordered to be written:

'The fortunate people from all lands, together with the people of Kalakh, have I entertained in splendour for ten days, refreshed with wine, bathed, anointed and heaped with every honour. Then I allowed them to depart in peace and good spirits.'

But the troops of his son Shalmaneser III, conqueror and king of Ashur (859–824 BC), advanced – so it is recorded – 'as far as the land of Khatti and up to the Great Sea where the sun does not set'. The Phoenician ports of Tyre, Sidon and Arpad were made to pay tribute. The Phoenician kings were compelled to bring the richest products of their country to the king of Ashur, and kiss his feet as a sign of submission. And the Israelite army under King Ahab, together with the armies of ten allied kings, suffered a crushing defeat near Qarqar in

Below left: King Sargon II (721–705 BC) – detail from the relief in the throne-room at Dur-Sharrukin (now Khorsabad) (Iraq Museum, Baghdad)
Opposite top left: Lion, one of the figures lining the processional way in Babylon – glazed brick (height: two feet nine inches), built between 604 and 562 BC (Near East Museum, Berlin)
Opposite top right: Bull from the processional way in Babylon – glazed brick (Near East Museum, Berlin)
Opposite bottom: Dragon from the processional way in Babylon (Near East Museum, Berlin)

northern Syria. In spite of this, Babylon secretly remained the spiritual capital.

A hundred years later Sargon II, king of Assyria (722–705 BC), built a new palace at Dur-Sharrukin in only six years. In 705 BC, when he was killed during a campaign in the Taurus mountains, the frontiers of his kingdom stretched from the mountains in the east across to Egypt.

His successor, Sennacherib, did not heed the word of Marduk, the god of Babylon. He destroyed the holy city in 689 BC, and commanded it to be written: 'I demolished the city and delivered it all to the flames. I wrought greater havoc than a flood. So that this city and the temples of its gods would never be found again, I made it like a swamp.'

He established the kingdom's new capital at Nineveh,

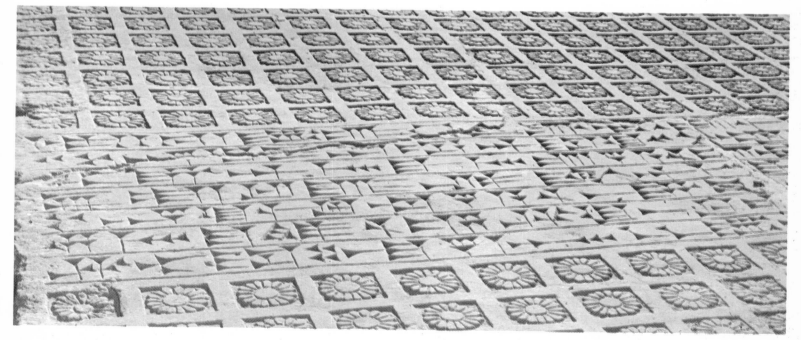

Below: Draw-well of ancient design in the desert near Til Barsip
Opposite: 'Babylonian map of the world' found at Sippar, probably dating from 2300 BC (British Museum, London)

today known as Quyunjiq, situated opposite Mosul on the left bank of the Tigris. And it continued as such under the 'great and famous Ashurbanipal', who led a cruel campaign against Egypt, founded a vast library, and had his life's work illustrated in reliefs carved on the palace walls. But the days of Nineveh and Ashur were numbered. Nahum, the Jewish prophet, warned:

'The Lord is slow to anger, and great in power, and will not at all acquit the wicked . . .

'Woe to the bloody city! it is all full of lies and robbery . . . the noise of a whip, and the noise of the rattling of the wheels, and of the prancing horses, and of the jumping chariots. The horseman lifteth up both the bright sword and the glittering spear: and there is a multitude of slain, and a great number of carcasses . . .

'Thy shepherds slumber, O king of Assyria: thy nobles shall dwell in the dust: thy people is scattered upon the mountains, and no man gathereth them.'

When Egypt, under King Psammetichus, succeeded in shaking off Assyrian rule, it was a sign for the Medes, a rough and warlike race of horsemen in Iran who had been held in bondage by the Assyrians for five hundred years, to form an alliance with the Chaldaeans, a Semitic people of southern Mesopotamia, under the leadership of their king Nabopolassar, and together smash the yoke of Ashur.

Ashur fell in 614 BC, Nineveh in 612, and the king and his people were overwhelmed. The subject peoples took merciless revenge: not one Assyrian city remained standing, and their inhabitants were cruelly massacred.

Mesopotamia's political structure was completely changed. A Median kingdom arose in the north with its capital at Ecbatana; it stretched almost to the borders of India. And in the south was the second Babylonian empire, with Babylon as its capital; it once again embraced the whole of Mesopotamia from Ur to the northern mountains and from the Persian Gulf to the shores of the Mediterranean.

The last great days of the neo-Babylonian kingdom began. The Babylonian map of the world displays the celestial and geographical cosmos: beneath the celestial pole, the seat of the highest god, lies Babylon, the link between heaven and earth. Both converge to form the hub of the world. Emanating from the town, the four quarters of the earth lie at the four points of the compass,

protected by four gods. Twelve countries are protected by the twelve signs of the zodiac in the heaven, which is in the form of a circle round the earth defining space and time. Campaign routes and the caravan trails are indicated by seven horn-like projections pointing out to the furthest distances.

In 587 Nebuchadnezzar II, king of Babylon (605–562 BC), took command of his army in order to destroy Israel, the former province of Assyria. He ordered it to be written: 'Nebuchadnezzar, the favourite of Marduk, the illustrious priest-prince, the prophesied, the first-born son of Nabopolassar, king of Babylon, am I.'

Jeremiah, the man from Judah, had prophesied: 'Woe unto thee, O Jerusalem! I have seen thine adulteries,

Above: Model of the processional way and Ishtar gate at Babylon (Near East Museum, Berlin)
Left: Reconstruction of the Ishtar gate of Babylon (Near East Museum, Berlin)

Below: Model of the city of Babylon as it was at the time of Nebuchadnezzar II (Babylon Museum)
Bottom: Disc-shaped miniature with inscription naming Nebuchadnezzar II, 604–562 BC (Near East Museum, Berlin)
Opposite: The temple of Ninmah at Babylon (reconstructed) – view from the cella out into the courtyard, with its cistern

and thy neighings, the lewdness of thy whoredom, and thine abominations on the hills in the fields . . .

'Thus saith the Lord unto me . . . I will appoint over them the sword to slay, and the dogs to tear . . .

'Therefore will I cast you out of this land into a land that ye know not, neither ye nor your fathers . . .

'I will deliver this city into the hands of Nebuchadnezzar king of Babylon . . . and he shall burn it with fire.'

And the Babylonian army destroyed the city of Jerusalem and its temple. Nebuchadnezzar himself put out the eyes of the king of Judah with a golden dagger, and led the Jewish people into captivity in Babylon. The Jews saw the power and the glory and the riches of Babylon, the heavenly city on the Euphrates. They read what Nebuchadnezzar had ordered to be written:

'Whereas Marduk created me according to the law to renew the cities, I in all reverence obeyed. Babylon, the city of my royal glory, I completed her great walls. At her gates I set mighty bulls and terrible dragons. I laid her foundations firmly on the bosom of the underworld, I built up her summit as high as a mountain. In Esagila, the palace of heaven and earth, I caused the dwelling-place of the gods' delight to be covered with glittering gold. I rebuilt the step-tower of Babylon.'

They saw the temple of Ninmah, goddess of fertility. And they heard the prayer: 'Merciful mother, spread forth my seed, make my tribe numerous.' They saw the king's castle with its countless rooms and the vast ten-thousand-square-foot room with halls for foreign ambassadors and kings, and the many chambers and apartments for the royal family and palace officials – the focus and shrine of temporal power. They saw the museum in which the king collected monuments of Babylonia's past and trophies from foreign lands. They heard the priests call out to the king: 'May the network of canals belong to you! May the pastures of the desert be yours! King, hold the sun in your right hand! King, hold the moon in your left hand! May the divine kingship penetrate your body!' They heard the temple bells chime when the caravans of horses and camels laden with rubies, purple, rugs, corals and pearls, gold and precious spices, arrived from Ecbatana in Iran, from the luxury-producing cities of Phoenicia, from the city of Sardis in the west of Asia Minor, the towns and villages of India and the cedar-forests of the Lebanon. And,

like a dream against the shimmering hot air of the boundless yellow desert, they saw the 'Hanging Gardens', the second of the Seven Wonders of the Ancient World and the one which has captured men's imaginations to an extent surpassed only by paradise and the Garden of Eden. Fischer von Erlach, for instance, the famous baroque master-builder (1656–1723), tried to produce an architecturally correct representation of the dream, using the details given in the ancient authors in his *Entwurff einer Historischen Architectur.*

In the sharply-angled north-east corner of the royal palace, near the vast Ishtar gate covered with blue glazed bricks and decorated with the emblems of the gods, Robert Koldewey discovered the foundations of the Hanging Gardens.

A huge block of stones comprising fourteen chambers with massive vaults, the entire structure lay beneath the ground-level of Nebuchadnezzar's palace. Thus they can only be the foundations, but they still give an idea of how big and impressive the upper structure must have been. The Greek Diodorus Siculus, who visited Babylon at the time of Caesar when the Hanging Gardens were still to be seen, records in his *Bibliotheca Historica*:

'And then there were the Hanging Gardens – *Paradeisos*. Going up to the top is like climbing a mountain. Each terrace rises up from the last like the syrinx, the pipes of Pan, which are made of several tubes of unequal length. This gives the appearance of a theatre. It was flanked by perfectly-constructed walls twenty-five feet thick. The galleries were roofed with stone balconies.

Above these there was first a bed of reeds with a great quantity of bitumen, then a double layer of baked bricks set in gypsum, then over that a covering of lead so that the moisture from the soil heaped above it would not seep through. The earth was deep enough to contain the roots of the many varieties of trees which fascinated the beholder with their great size and their beauty.

'There was also a passage which had pipes leading up to the highest level and machinery for raising water through which great quantities of water were drawn from the river, with none of the process being visible from the outside.'

Herodotus, the father of history, states that the creator of the Hanging Gardens was Sammuramat or Semiramis, wife of Shamshi-Adad and mother of

Adadnirari, king of the four corners of the earth, who in about 850 BC recorded of herself that: 'In the midst of my politics and my wars I found time to satisfy the desires of my body.'

Alongside the Hanging Gardens, the processional way, lined with lifesize statues of mythical beasts, leads up to the Ishtar gate, which was decorated with 575 multicoloured figures of bulls and dragons. Here, according to Herodotus, up to a million men and women came to pray during the days of Ishtar's festival.

In Babylon, as in Ur and Ashur, she ruled over the priest-king, to whom she 'consigned the staff and ring, the symbols of power'; she ruled over the free citizens, who, although subject to the law, were nobody's personal property, and formed the top rank of society; she

Left: Façade of the throne-room at the royal palace of Babylon at the time of Nebuchadnezzar II – coloured glazed brick (height: forty-one feet) (Near East Museum, Berlin)
Opposite above: View of Babylon's processional way as it is today; it traversed the ancient city from north to south
Opposite below: The present-day remains of the throne-room in Nebuchadnezzar II's citadel at Babylon

ruled over the slaves, who owed their condition to birth or captivity, and went, like cattle, by the names of their owners, and built the cities, palaces and temples; she ruled over the priests, whose temples were not only places of worship but also centres for all civic, commercial and intellectual activities. They managed the huge estates, ran industries and trained the scribes and officials. They fostered the sciences: mathematics, astronomy, languages, medicine, state and economic law, diplomacy, architecture, technology.

But fate imposes a time limit on men and nations. Babylon was great, it seemed, and its king all-powerful: it had confined the Jewish people within its borders, the Chaldaeans' fist lay heavily on Egypt, and the war-chariots rolled far beyond the borders.

But Babylon brought retribution upon itself. Its king pleaded: 'Lord, my offences are many, great are my sins. Have mercy on my miserable body, which is full of sickness and confusion. Have mercy on my anguished heart, which is filled with tears and sighs.' The priests accused: 'Nebuchadnezzar has sinned, and invoked the wrath of the gods. The gods are waiting upon the sinner's death, to restore the balance between good and evil through his punishment.' And the king himself foretold: 'A Persian mule will come and enslave you. I, Nebuchadnezzar, prophesy disaster for you Babylonians.'

And the Jews sat beside the Euphrates and rejoiced: 'Your end has come, and your power is no more.' And the 'Persian mule', King Cyrus of the Achaemenids,

advanced with his army while Nebuchadnezzar was dying.

With the victory of the Persians in 539 BC, Babylon's political independence was finally lost for ever.

Alexander the Great's intention to make Babylon the capital of his newly founded world empire was never realised, for he died of a fever in this very city in 323 BC.

The memory of the power and greatness of Ur, Ashur and Babylon remained, however, never to fade. And – as if to atone for all the cruelty – the memory of the Hanging Gardens of Semiramis.

Detail from the colossal relief in the throne-room of King Sargon II at Dur-Sharrukin (Iraq Museum, Baghdad)

The Zeus of Olympia

Homer gives us this description of Zeus, the lord of the thunderclouds, in the first book of the *Iliad*: 'The son of Cronus spoke, and nodded his dark brow, and the ambrosial locks waved from the king's immortal head: the heights of Olympus trembled.'

With the statue of Zeus at Olympia, completed in 433 BC, the sculptor Phidias personified the concept of God and the divine as the object of every Greek's longing for perfection. Not to have seen the Olympian Zeus, therefore, was regarded as unholy. The statue rightly came to be included among the Seven Wonders of the World. But its origins lie in a far remoter time.

Hesiod, the first poet on European soil and, after Homer, the greatest of the Greek epic writers, gives this account in his genealogy of the gods, the *Theogony*.

Below: Head of Gaea, 300 BC, found at Zarcos in Thessaly (Istanbul Museum)
Opposite: Zeus of Ionnina – bronze (Istanbul Museum)

In the beginning was Chaos, yawning and boundless space; which, made fertile by Erebus, the darkness, bore the mighty Gaea, the earth, broad-bosomed; from her sprang Uranus, the starry sky, and Pontus, the roaring surge of the sea.

But it was Gaea still who nourished all creatures in the sea, on the hallowed soil of the earth, and in the air.

Moved by Eros, god of love, Gaea joined with Uranus and bore the Titans, her mighty sons and daughters: Oceanus, the stream of the world; Tethys, the life-giving moisture, the mother of springs and rivers; Hyperion, creator of the sun, the moon and the dawn; and the wily Cronus, who hated his vigorous father Uranus. Gaea also bore him the one-eyed Cyclopes, in whose works were strength, power and invention.

When they became too powerful for Uranus, he threw them deep in the bosom of the earth, into Tartarus, the gloomy prison of the Titans in the underworld. But Gaea, the giant earth, groaned within herself: 'O children, take vengeance on your own father for this brutal outrage.' And Cronus, mighty in cunning, castrated and killed his father. But from the dead god's blood sprang the Erinyes, the goddesses of inexorable revenge, and the race of Giants.

Then Zeus, the son of Cronus, set out with some of the Titans to overthrow his father. Olympus, Greece's highest mountain, became his stronghold, and Thessaly his battlefield. Cronus fell, and Zeus became ruler of the world. He set Hades, his brother, and his wife Persephone to rule over the underworld. Dark-haired Poseidon, his other brother, the earthshaker, he made ruler of the sea. Zeus himself chose Olympus for his throne, to wield the highest power over heaven, earth and sea.

Then the Giants, sprung from the blood of Uranus, rose up against the new gods to seize their power over heaven and earth. But Zeus, hurling lightning, struck them down. In Zeus, the mightiest of the gods, there henceforth dwelt the highest wisdom in the world, the harmony of heaven and the rule of law on earth.

Earthly rulers received their power from Zeus, the king of kings, and he was author and protector of the freedom of the nations. Zeus lived with the gods on Olympus in eternal youth. On the eternally snow-covered summit of the mountain in Thessaly, overlooking the Aegean Sea, Hephaestus, son of Zeus and the

god of fire, famous for his wisdom, built the palaces of the gods. Hera lived there, the dark-eyed wife of Zeus, enthroned on a golden throne, the immortal queen of the heavens and protectress of mothers. Athena also, protectress of men, the embodiment of wise counsel, sprung from the head of Zeus; and Apollo, the healer and punisher, with his twin sister Artemis, the mighty huntress and goddess of nature.

Aphrodite, garlanded with gold, goddess of love and immortal beauty, born from the foam of the sea; Hermes, the messenger of the gods, the bringer of blessings; Ares, mighty with the javelin, the king of manly courage; and Dionysus, crowned with ivy and garlanded with vines, the god of singers.

Rarely is the summit of Olympus altogether free of

150

clouds, for its custodians, the blithe and lovely-haired Horae, carefully close the portals of the mountain with golden clouds, and open them only when a god goes forth. From here Zeus sets the clouds in motion, stirs up the storms, releases the thunder and hurls forth the lightning.

He weighs men's fates in the balance, and keeps watch over families and assemblies in council. He defends the sanctity of oaths, and of hospitality to travellers. Only Zeus knows the future of all beings. In the storm, in the flight of birds, in dreams and in the rustling of the trees in the oak-groves he conveys his will to mankind.

At Dodona, near the lake of Ionnina, stood the oldest of the sanctuaries dedicated to Zeus. Dodona is bordered on the west by the Ionian Sea, named after Io, the beautiful priestess of Hera of Argos, with whom Zeus fell in love; on the east by fertile and well-watered Thessaly, home of the swiftest and bravest horses; in the north by mountainous Illyria, the vast pasture-land for cattle, sheep and goats; and in the south by the rich wine country of Aetolia, with its warlike and rapacious fighting-men. The priestesses of Dodona used to sing: 'Zeus was, Zeus is and Zeus ever shall be; O Zeus, greatest of the gods.'

Dione, daughter of Oceanus and Tethys, became the wife of Zeus of Dodona and mother of Aphrodite, the goddess of love and beauty. Zeus made his pronouncements known to all Greeks through the voice of his son Apollo, 'the stalwart youth, his curly locks flowing

about his broad shoulders, who was like a star on the bright midday.' This took place at Delphi, in the centre of Greece, set in the district of Phocis, at the navel of the world, where the god's eagles from the east and the west had met. Delphi, where the winged horse Pegasus struck open the Castalian spring from the rocks of Parnassus with a hoof-beat, releasing the waters that inspired to song the poets who drank them; where the twelve tribes of the land, ignoring their different origins, formed an alliance together – the Amphictyony – and held courts of justice; where, during the Pythian Games, founded almost seven hundred years before the birth of Christ, the poets would gather in the theatre to compete with songs in honour of Apollo Musagetes; where the charioteers battled for victory in the thousand-

foot-long hippodrome on the nearby plain of Crisa, and athletes competed for the victor's laurels in noble sports in the stadium – here at Delphi, Pythia, the priestess of Apollo, sat on a golden tripod above a crevice which gave out intoxicating vapours and, inspired by them, murmured mysterious words which the priests interpreted to those who had come to consult the oracle.

For Phoebus Apollo had proclaimed: 'O ye foolish mortals, weighed down with sorrows, whose hearts are always visited by troubles and distress and heavy oppression: I can easily bring you help, take my words to heart.'

'See,' sang the poet, 'Helios shines down now over the earth with his glittering chariot. The stars in the holy

Opposite: View of the valley of the Plistus river at Delphi from the temple of Apollo
Below: The *omphalos*, the 'navel of the world', from the precinct of the temple at Delphi (Delphi Museum)
Right: Caryatid from the treasury of Siphnos at Delphi (Delphi Museum)

Left: Ancient stonework surrounding the 'Castalian spring' at Delphi, the fountain of the Muses
Below: The altar of the temple of Apollo at Delphi

night flee before the fire of heaven. The untrodden heights of Parnassus are aglow with light, touched by the day that is breaking for the mortals. The withering fragrance of myrrh drifts up to Phoebus's rafters. The woman of Delphi is enthroned on the holy tripod and sings out to the Greeks the judgment that Apollo sounded about her.

'Men of Delphi, servants of Phoebus, rise! Go to the silver-sparkling stream of Castalia, sprinkle your limbs with the pure dew, then climb up to the temple and hallow your mouths with pious words. And if any approach who seek counsel, address them healing words in the appropriate tongue.'

In this way Zeus ordered and admonished the whole of Greece. Whoever opposed the laws and command-ments of the shepherd of the peoples was punished with the wrath of Apollo. With his arrows, which he shot from a silver bow, the far-striker would seek out the wrongdoer and bring him death and destruction.

In the days when men still hunted lions in Greece and Mesopotamia, and took down Homer's verses about the Trojan war and the life and death of heroes, and the adventurous return of the cunning Odysseus to Ithaca, the various Greek tribes already felt themselves to be one people as distinct from the barbarians around them. They built their houses round the temple of a communal god and set up walls to protect them. As early as the seventh century BC, such cities as Athens, Sparta, Corinth, Thebes and Miletus had begun to flourish and assume importance in the fertile valleys

and on the islands of Greece. The Greeks cultivated wheat and barley with ox, ass and plough. Olives and vines were grown with industry and skill.

The Greeks had learnt spinning and weaving from the women of the Nile. They had also acquired the twelve divisions of the day and the secrets of the heavens by way of Egypt from the Babylonians. The Phoenicians taught them navigation along the sea-coasts. Before long the Greeks had settled on the shores of the Black Sea, in Sicily and in southern Italy, and Marseilles – known as Massalia – was a Greek city.

From the middle of the seventh century BC, in every Greek city coins were soon being struck. The primitive system of trading by exchange was thus superseded.

The *polis*, the urban community, the state, contained

Below: Relief showing the Pythian tripod and two griffins, located in the region of the theatre at Miletus
Bottom left: Head of the bronze votive statue of a charioteer (height: five foot eleven inches) found at Delphi, dating from the year 474 BC (Delphi Museum)
Bottom right: Head of the god Apollo, found at Delphi (Delphi Museum)
Opposite: Bronze head of a lion, Olympia

many different elements which exercised authority: the people, the aristocracy, party-leaders and tyrants – but never the semi-divine monarchs surrounded by a ceremonial court who ruled over Egypt and Mesopotamia.

The world in those days comprised Greece, Egypt, Asia Minor and Syria, the Caucusus as far as the Caspian Sea, the Babylonian and old Assyrian kingdoms, Media and Persia, and stretched on as far as the Indus. And all the nations inhabiting this world paid tribute to Darius, ruler of Persia, the King of Kings. The ruling heart of this world beat in the cities of Persepolis, Susa and Ecbatana.

Only the European Greeks, Italy, Carthage, Sicily and the Phoenician colonies of Spain were not under compulsion to pay tribute to the Persian empire; they

Below: The palace of Darius at Persepolis
Opposite: Stele showing an armed runner (known as the Marathon runner) at the point of collapsing at the finishing-line (height: three feet four inches), from about 520 BC (National Museum, Athens)

kept peace with it, however. The only threat to the empire came from the Scythian hordes of southern Russia and Central Asia. In the barracks of Persepolis, the famous 'Ten Thousand' were ready.

In the year 513 BC Darius ordered his troops to march beyond the Bosphorus through Bulgaria and beyond the Danube far into the north. Thrace and Macedonia were subjugated.

The Greek cities of Asia Minor rose up against Persian rule, and the Greeks of Europe lent them their support. In 490 BC Miltiades, a brave man and one of the *strategi* (military commanders) of Athens, led a small army in a pitched battle against overwhelming Persian forces on the narrow plain of Marathon on the east coast of Attica.

Below: Façade of the tombs of the Achaemenids at Naqsh-i-Rustam, Iran
Opposite: Youth with victor's headband – bronze head from the fifth century BC (Glyptothek, Munich)

160

Then Darius, the king of kings, ordered an imperial campaign against the Greeks. But he died in 486, before he could place his troops on the march.

In Naqsh-i-Rustam, the burial ground of the Achaemenid kings, he found his last resting-place. Six years later, his son Xerxes led the army across the Bosphorus to Greece.

Themistocles, the commander of the Greek army, demanded the surrender of Thessaly and a combined land and sea operation at Thermopylae, the gateway to Central Greece. The Spartans, who were competing with Athens at this time, demanded as the price for their co-operation the surrender of Central Greece and defence of the Isthmus. The Persians took advantage of the quarrel: Leonidas and his small troop of Spartans were

Below: The Hill of Cronus, rising a hundred feet above the Altis at Olympia – probably the oldest centre for the worship of Zeus in the region of Elis
Bottom: The sanctuary of Pelops in the middle of the Altis at Olympia
Opposite below: Model of the east pediment of the temple of Zeus at Olympia, showing the probable arrangement of the sculptured figures
Opposite bottom left: Head of an old man (known as the seer) from the east pediment of the temple of Zeus at Olympia (Olympia Museum)
Opposite bottom right: Statue of the charioteer Myrtilus from the east pediment of the temple of Zeus at Olympia (Olympia Museum)

wiped out by the Persians at Thermopylae, and Athens went up in flames.

Themistocles only just managed to rally the Greek ships before engaging the Persian fleet at Salamis and winning a complete victory.

In 479 BC, under Pausanias of Sparta, who commanded the combined Greek armies, the much-feared Persian cavalry was destroyed at Plataea, and the infantry put to flight.

Xerxes returned to Asia. His world empire was shaken to its foundations by uprisings in Egypt, Syria and Media. Nike, the victory-goddess, the personification of victory, poised over Greece and made her dwelling in Olympia, the city which, according to legend, was founded by Hercules, the lion-hearted son

of Zeus, after many battles and wanderings. He measured out the site for Zeus's sanctuary, built the surrounding wall, and laid down the rules and procedure for the Olympic Games.

The Olympic Games were recorded from 776 BC, and special treaties ensured that all conflicts among men and city-states should be suspended when the Greeks came together to compete at Olympia beneath the far-seeing eye of Zeus.

No armed band could enter the sanctuary, the Altis. And a perpetual truce reigned in the flourishing land of Elis. Every four years the messengers hurried out of Olympia to proclaim the time of peace throughout Greece. Time was measured in Olympiads, and distances in *stadia*, the length of the Olympic stadium.

Olympia consisted of two completely distinct sections. On the Altis, the grove and temple precinct of the Olympian Zeus, bordered by the waters of the Alpheus and Cladeus rivers, was situated only what belonged to the gods. The other part was for men and their day-to-day affairs.

In the centre of the Altis is the Pelopium, the tomb and sanctuary of Pelops, a grandson of Zeus.

The east pediment of the temple of Zeus shows the contest between Pelops, the horse-tamer, and King Oenomaus of Elis, who had promised his beloved daughter Hippodamia only to the man who could beat him in a chariot-race; no one could do so, however, for his father, the god Ares, had given him horses that were 'faster than the north wind'.

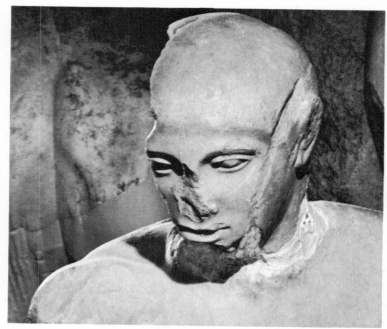

Myrtilus, King Oenomaus's charioteer, bribed by Pelops, loosened the wheels of his master's chariot. Pelops triumphed, and became king of Elis. With Hippodamia he began the line of Atrides, who were to include King Agamemnon and Menelaus.

The oldest temple building at Olympia was the Heraeum, the sanctuary of Hera of the golden throne, the wife of Zeus; it had six columns across the front and sixteen along its sides. Beneath its sacred statue was said to be stored the original charter of the Olympic Games. In one of the niches of the temple stood the statue of Hermes, messenger of the gods and the son of Zeus, the god of success and prosperity. Its sculptor was Praxiteles, the great master of Athens. Miraculously it has been preserved.

Below left: Statue of Hermes, the original sculpture by Praxiteles, which stood in a niche in the temple of Hera at Olympia – fourth century BC (Olympia Museum)
Below right: The temple of Hera at Olympia, first built in the seventh century BC, but several times re-modelled
Opposite: Hera of Olympia – limestone (height: twenty inches) dating from about 600 BC (Olympia Museum)

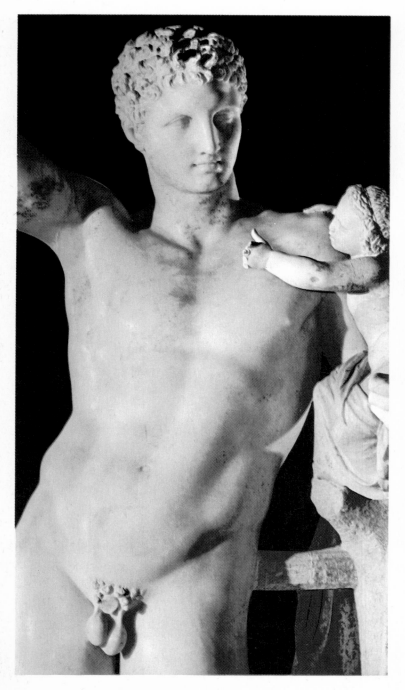

Zeus, the shepherd of the peoples, the perfecter, was for centuries revered beneath the blue sky and the rustling trees of Olympia. The ground was covered with such objects as enormous three-legged cauldrons – votive offerings of the faithful, the sign of child-like devotion and self-sacrifice – and griffins' heads of all sizes, to ward off evil forces. On the walls of the stadium were placed victory monuments made of captured weapons.

In about 470 BC, building began on the temple to the god Zeus.

Fifteen years later, in about 456, it was already completed. It was 210 feet long and 90 feet wide. Rising above three lofty steps, there were thirteen columns along the sides and six across the front, each more than

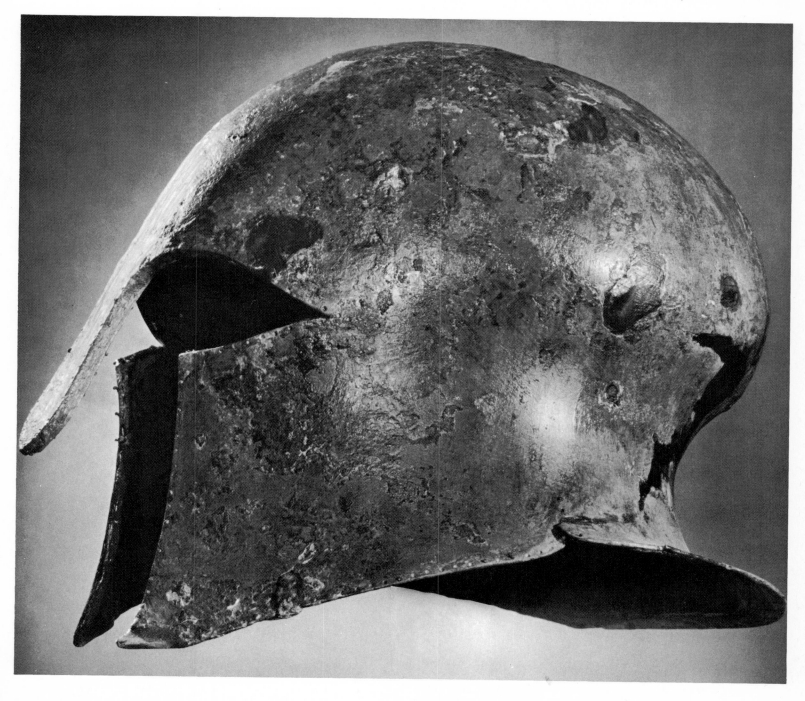

Below left: The steps of the temple of Zeus at Olympia
Below right: Remains of the cella of the temple of Zeus at Olympia
Bottom: The columns of the temple of Zeus at Olympia, brought down by an earthquake
Opposite below: A reconstruction of the temple of Zeus at Olympia, published in 1864, showing a cross-section through the cella and giving a view of the statue of Zeus
Opposite bottom: Longitudinal section, drawn to scale, through the temple of Zeus at Olympia, published in 1864

thirty-two feet high and over six feet in diameter. No temple in Greece had mightier columns than these.

The porous surface of the shell limestone with which the temple was built was covered with a coat of fine stucco, creating the impression of glistening marble.

There were fifty-one gargoyles in the shape of lions' heads to drain rainwater from the marble-tiled roof. The controlled *ethos* of the east pediment, which shows Zeus, the guardian and protector of oaths, is set in contrast to the unrestrained *pathos* of the west pediment, on which Apollo is depicted as arbitrator between barbarian savageness and Greek order.

The battle is raging between the Lapiths, human giants under their king Pirithous, who is about to celebrate his wedding to Didamia, and the Centaurs, a

company of wild and drunken creatures in whom horse and rider have grown into one body, and who provoked the battle when they tried to assault the women and boys among the wedding-guests.

Apollo stands in the centre – as the son of Zeus, he is the guardian and protector of divine order. Quietly and protectively stretching out his right hand towards the threatened bride, he accords victory to Greek culture over barbarian strength.

Above the six columns of the front and back porches of the temple were portrayed the twelve labours of Hercules that he performed in the service of King Eurystheus. The young hero stands exhausted over the 'invulnerable' lion of Nemea, which he strangled with his bare hands.

Athena, the daughter of Zeus, points out to Hercules the Stymphalian birds which, until he slew them, had terrorised Arcadia with their brazen claws and beaks and their feathers which they shot out like arrows. The Cretan bull, which Poseidon had brought forth from the sea and ordered King Midas to sacrifice, Hercules captured alive.

When Hercules, given the task of fetching the golden apples of the Hesperides, was unable to find them, he carried the heavens for the giant Atlas, who had promised to bring them to him. The goddess Athena stood by the hero. When Atlas returned with the apples, Hercules cunningly persuaded the giant to shoulder his burden once again.

Dragging Cerberus, the three-headed hell-hound, out

Below: Model of the west pediment of the temple of Zeus at Olympia (Olympia Museum)
Bottom row: Original surviving sculptures from this pediment
Left: Head of a reclining figure
Left centre: Centaur and Lapith
Right centre: Female Lapith
Right: Female Lapith

from the underworld to bring before Eurystheus was Hercules' most difficult task. To complete his twelve labours, Hercules breached the rocks with a mighty thrust to divert the Alpheus and Peneus rivers through the stables of Augias, king of Elis, and so clean away the dung of the giant herds. When Augias refused to give the hero his reward, Hercules, under the protection of Athena, made war on Elis, became its king, instituted the Olympic Games in honour of Zeus enthroned in the clouds, and founded the sacred grove. On the peak of the temple roof, above the pediments, stood gilt statues of Nike, the work of Paeonius.

The temple of Zeus was destroyed by two severe earthquakes in the years 523 and 551 AD, but some indication of how it may have appeared and the impression

it created is given by the temple of Apollo at nearby Bassae. One wall of the cella that enclosed the statue is still standing, as are the surrounding columns. The architrave, the stone beams that supported the roof and pediments, is still in place above the capitals. And we can still observe how the beauty and grandeur of the building blend with the tranquillity of nature to form a unified whole.

At Olympia, three steps led up to a broad portico beyond which was the vestibule of the inner temple. The cella, or temple building proper, the home of the god, which housed the most famous artistic works of antiquity, is still easily distinguishable by its ruins. The entire length of the interior was bordered on either side by rows of columns arranged in two tiers, which gave

visitors a direct view of the forty-foot-high ivory and gold statue of Zeus situated in the adjoining chamber. This Wonder of the World is believed to have been taken to Constantinople in about 394 AD after the dissolution of the sanctuary in the late classical period, and there destroyed.

Nevertheless, the description given by the geographer Pausanias, who lived at the time of the emperor Hadrian, allows us to form a fairly accurate picture of Phidias's statue of Zeus; it was this, in fact, that prompted Fischer von Erlach and others to design reconstructions of it.

The god sat on a cedarwood throne, which rested on a vast pedestal adorned with the full range of Olympian deities flanked by Helios and Selene, as if to present an

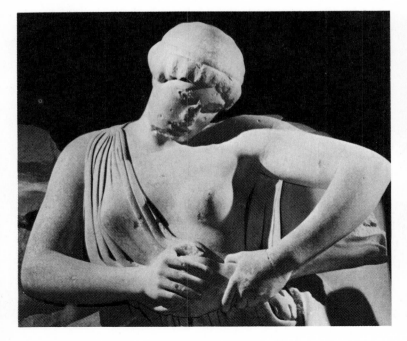

image of Olympus itself. The actual chair of the throne was laid out and ornamented with ebony, ivory, gold and precious stones. Around its legs were dancing goddesses of victory. Charites and Horae hovered at the top of the backrest about the head of their father Zeus. The stool that supported his feet was carried by two golden lions. The head, torso and other unclad parts of the body, including the feet, were made of ivory. The eyes were probably glittering gemstones. The hair of the head and beard was made of pure gold, as was the statue of Nike, poised with an olive-branch, which the god carried on his outstretched right hand. The sceptre which he held in his left hand, symbol of his rule over earth, and which shone with every colour of the rainbow, was made of an alloy of various precious

Opposite: The figure of Apollo which, from its central position, dominates the scene depicted on the west pediment of the temple of Zeus (Olympia Museum)
Right: Head of Apollo – detail from the foregoing

Below: Metope from the temple of Zeus at Olympia: Atlas brings the golden apples of the Hesperides to Hercules, who is meanwhile supporting the heavens for him
Opposite: The temple of Apollo at Bassae, situated at a height of 3,700 feet, completed in about 400 BC

metals. Perched on the sceptre was an eagle. The garment that draped the lower part of the figure was also made of gold, and covered with flowers made from a kind of enamel.

In Phidias's workshop at Olympia were found a large number of moulds for casting both the gold robe and its ornamentation. There were even portions of the same enamel substance, shavings of ivory, tools, an earthenware mug with Phidias's personal inscription, and the fragments of a pot which depicted the invoking of daemonic forces by the 'master' and his 'assistants'.

The rediscovered workshop corresponds exactly in its proportions, in the direction it faces, and hence in its lighting, with the cella of the temple of Zeus. The statue of Zeus, which Phidias worked on for eight years there,

could thus be taken out of the workshop complete and set up within the inner chamber of the temple of Zeus which stood opposite.

Phidias, the creator of the Olympian Zeus, who is said to have portrayed himself on the shield of the statue of Athena in the Parthenon as an old man lifting up a stone (we have a copy of it dating from Roman times), was a very close personal friend of the great Athenian statesman Pericles.

His early work, an Apollo, standing naked and serene, with slender cheeks and full lips, and a severity that is consciously brought close to the sublime, is the greatest portrayal of the divine that we know in ancient art from our own direct experience.

Phidias, with his head of the poet Anacreon – it has survived in the form of a copy – had already developed the particular classical type that was to achieve its fullest expression in the Olympian Zeus. Very much akin to it is the Zeus with ram's horns, the nobility of which outweighs the monstrous element.

The large Elean commemorative coin struck during the time of the emperor Hadrian gives us some indication of what Phidias had expressed in the face and figure of the Zeus of Olympia, what it was that made their highest god seem a real and living presence to the Greeks, and what it was that they employed like a magic remedy against all the afflictions of this world.

Dion Chrysostom of Prusa describes it to us thus: 'The strength and nobility of the royal ruler of the world, the kind and friendly nature of the father and

provider, the stern dignity of the patron of the *polis* and the law, the benevolent humanity of the protector of foreigners and exiles, of friends and all who entreat protection, and the simplicity and magnanimity of the augmenter of possessions and of fertility.'

The Greek city-states also placed their treasure under the protection of Zeus. On a terrace at the northern boundary of the Altis, facing the temple of Zeus, stood twelve *thesauri*, or treasuries, of which the foundations and substructure are still preserved. The treasure itself has vanished. Located separately from the others is the treasury of the Macedonians, the Philippeum, a circular building with eighteen columns that housed the precious ivory and gold statues of Alexander the Great and his ancestors.

Below left: Obverse of the Elean coin from the time of the emperor Hadrian (117–138 AD) showing the head of Zeus with a laurel-wreath, probably based on Phidias's statue (British Museum, London)
Below right: Reverse side of a tetradrachm minted in Macedonia, showing Zeus enthroned with eagle and sceptre (British Museum, London)
Opposite: Head of Zeus, from a group in painted clay portraying the carrying off of Ganymede, found at Olympia – from about 470 BC (Olympia Museum)

But the temple and the Zeus of Olympia belonged to the entire Greek nation.

Every four years, in August or September, Greeks from the mainland, the Ionian islands and the settlements on the coasts of Asia and Africa, Italy, Sicily and Gaul would come together around Zeus. The palaestra, or wrestling school, situated to the north-west of the Altis was where wrestlers and boxers carried on their training. The gymnasium, attached to the palaestra, was for the use of runners and discus and javelin throwers. Here, too, were the lodgings where the athletes stayed during the games.

On the first day of the competitions the athletes took an oath before Zeus, the protector of vows, that they would be guilty of no dishonesty or wrongdoing during

Below: The shield of Athena from the Parthenon in Athens – Roman copy of the original, which has been destroyed. The bare-headed figure of an old man with arms raised (lower left) is said to be a self-portrait by Phidias (British Museum, London)
Opposite: Discobolus – a bronze statuette (9½ inches high) copied in Roman times from Myron's statue of the fifth century BC (Glyptothek, Munich)

the sacred contest. On the second day the competitions themselves began with prayers to Zeus and the drawing of lots, and went on for four days in all.

Through a covered way on the west side, headed by the purple-robed umpires – the *Hellanodikai* – the contestants entered the stadium, of which the drainage channel, still in existence today, measures six hundred Olympic feet (equivalent to 625 feet 6 inches) in length. When the umpires had taken their seats, the herald opened the games with the sacred declamation: 'Now Agon reigns, the lord of the glorious games, and Kairos, the god of the opportune moment, calls for there to be no more delay. Go now and engage your opponent so that it may be decided between you. But where victory finally goes will rest with Zeus.' In running, jumping,

wrestling and boxing, throwing the discus and the javelin, each contestant had to prove himself by his power of limb and determination of character.

What had once been patriotism became political intrigue. The child-like love of the gods changed to cold calculation. In place of bold adventurers and lion-hearted heroes there appeared cold-hearted merchants who bought their fame and glory. And the gods covered their heads.

When Phidias was working on the statue of Athena for the Parthenon at Athens, a building which he had influenced architecturally and for which he had produced the friezes, he was accused of embezzling gold that he had received for the statue. The kind of persons who had no interests beyond making money won the day. There is very little doubt that Phidias died in prison in Athens. Pericles, the leader of the Athenian state and Phidias's patron, was likewise accused of embezzling state funds, and overthrown. His beautiful mistress Aspasia, a connoisseur of the arts, succumbed, like Pericles, to fever and the plague.

Thirty years later the wise Socrates, a friend of them both, was obliged to drink the poisoned cup, accused of 'impiety and corruption of the young'.

When the young Alexander appeared on the scene it seemed that the scales had once again risen in mankind's favour. But his life was too short.

The time came when Roman generals plundered Olympia to acquire money and power. Nero debased Olympia by making it the setting for those frivolous

spectacles; emperors and millionaires put up baths and other buildings that served nothing but their own luxury. The Roman emperors at Byzantium dismantled the temples at Olympia in order to build defensive walls against the barbarians out of their stones. And in 393 AD the Olympic Games were declared pagan, and banned. Phidias's Zeus, for centuries the most sacred and majestic statue in Greece, was dragged off to Byzantium. And in 426 AD, by decree of the emperor, the temple of Zeus was set on fire.

What escaped destruction at men's hands was brought down by the earthquakes which occurred in the sixth century.

But as long as men live, the splendour of the Zeus of Olympia, its truth and beauty, will never die away.

Hera, Zeus and Hebe, their daughter – Greco-Roman relief (Louvre, Paris)

The Temple of Artemis at Ephesus

I have seen Babylon –
Chariots riding upon
Its wall,
High gardens' overfall –
The Colossus of the sun
And Zeus Olympian;
Marvelling at all:
How high Mausolus is hid
I know, and each Pyramid.

But when I'd seen
Where Artemis's
Temple kisses
The clouds, these lost their sheen:
This side of Heaven, I swear,
Sun gains no sight so fair.

ANTIPATER OF SIDON

'Of Artemis I sing, whose shafts are of gold, the loud, wild, pure maiden, the terror of the stags, who delights in her bow. Over the shadowy hills and windy peaks she draws her golden bow, rejoicing in the chase, and sends forth grievous shafts. But then she slackens her bow and hurries away to order the lovely dance of the Charites and Muses. Arrayed with precious golden jewels, she leads the chorus.'

Shrines were built to the goddess thus celebrated by Homer from Greece to the west of Asia Minor, and she was worshipped by Greeks, Asians and Romans. In the city of Ephesus on the west coast of Asia Minor stood the largest and most magnificent of her temples, the Artemision, which had been included since antiquity among the Seven Wonders of the World.

Opposite: Temple of Artemis, Hellenistic period, at Sardis, the one-time residential city of King Croesus of Lydia
Below left: Statue of Artemis, known as the Artemis of Gabii, ascribed to Praxiteles (Louvre, Paris)
Below right: The Artemis of Versailles, ascribed to the sculptor Leochares, dating from about 360 BC (Louvre, Paris)

The Acropolis of Athens, with its beautiful buildings and votive gifts to Athena, goddess of the city; it was laid waste by the Persians in 480 BC, but afterwards rebuilt and enlarged, particularly under Pericles

From the acropolises of the mainland the Greeks looked out over the deep-blue Aegean, flooded with sunlight, across the magic world of the Aegean islands towards the rich and mysterious lands of Asia Minor, and very soon felt the call of travel and adventure.

As early as 1000 or 2000 BC the boldest amongst them had travelled across to the Aegean islands, tilled the soil and bred cattle in the way they had been accustomed to at home, and implanted Hellenic religion and culture in their new world. They pushed on as far as Asia Minor, where they settled in the fertile valleys and round the estuaries of the principal rivers such as the Granicus, the Cayster and the Maeander.

When they journeyed inland they came upon fortified cities such as Gordium with royal palaces and temples

to the great mother-goddesses of Asia, which they took over and fused with their own ways and beliefs.

One of these strongholds, the old and wealthy city of Sardis, the seat of the kings of Lydia in the centre of western Asia Minor, situated on the northern slopes of Mount Tmolus on the banks of the gold-bearing Pactolus, resisted the conquering influx from Greece. Sardis was the abode of the goddess Ma, also called Cybele, the Great Mother of Asia, nourisher of all creatures, mistress of mountains and forests, both begetter and conceiver in one.

She made women into men – called Amazons – who founded cities and waged war, armed with battleaxe and spear, shield, quiver and bow. In their service even the mighty and lion-hearted Hercules became like a woman.

The mouth of the River Cayster; here, before the coastline had extended further out to sea, stood the ancient city of Ephesus, now known as Seljuk

Sardis – in whose fortress King Croesus of Lydia, of the dynasty of Mermnads, collected the treasures of the world – secured control of the Greek colonial cities in Asia Minor in the second half of the sixth century BC. Croesus also marched against the Greek port of Ephesus on the eastern shore of the blue Aegean at the mouth of the Cayster, the fish-laden river of which the fertile valley, the Asia prata, has given its name to the whole of Asia.

Artemis, the tall-towering, wonderful to see, the night-roaming goddess who stormed loud and wild through the hills, blazing torches in her hands, accompanied by a pair of magnificent hounds and a band of lovely nymphs, she, the pure maiden who delighted in her arrows, became goddess and patroness of Ephesus.

Below left: Ruins of a town gate in the ancient Phrygian city of Gordium, dating from about the eighth century BC
Below right: Remains of the acropolis of Sardis
Opposite: Relief of Cybele, the mother-goddess of Phrygia, carved in the rocks at Magnesia ad Sipylum

Below: Hercules with two warriors – fragments of relief from a frieze at the temple of Artemis at Magnesia ad Maeandrum
Bottom: Inscription of King Croesus from the archaic temple of Artemis at Ephesus, to which the fabulously rich king of Lydia made important contributions (British Museum, London)
Opposite (left): Ivory miniature of a lion, a votive offering from the temple of Artemis at Ephesus (Istanbul Museum)
Opposite (right): Ivory miniature of a goddess, a votive offering from the temple of Artemis at Ephesus (Istanbul Museum)

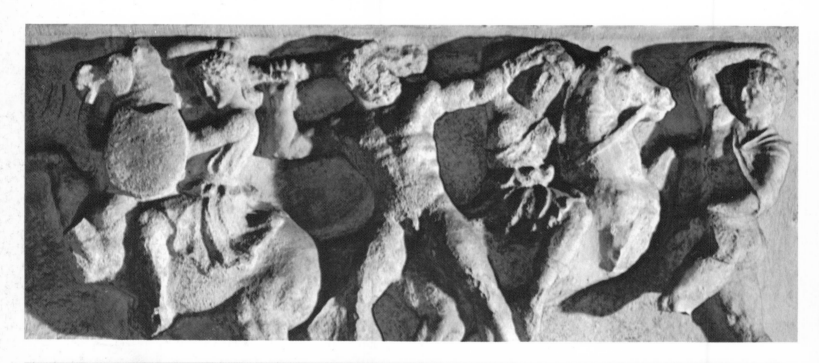

Another sanctuary besides hers belonged to Apollo, the mighty archer, who drew forth soothing music from the bowstring, the immortal god of number and proportion, whose clear sight penetrated the depths. Apollo and Artemis were the twin children of Zeus and the golden-haired Titaness Leto, born in the sacred grove of Ortygia near Ephesus.

When Croesus, the king of Lydia, added Ephesus to his kingdom after a short struggle, he bowed low before the sanctuary of Artemis, which, from about 550 BC, was being rebuilt on the site of an archaic temple according to the plans and under the supervision of the architect Chersiphron of Cnossus and his son Metagenes. A passage in the works of Herodotus, the historian and traveller from Halicarnassus, has preserved for us the

text of a dedicatory inscription on one of the columns stating that the majority of the sanctuary's sculptured columns were the gift of King Croesus. A great many of the gifts dedicated to the temple, including some thus presented by the king, have survived to our own day.

The temple of Artemis stood at the edge of the sea by a deep bay which in the course of 2,500 years became more and more filled up by land. Today the sacred precinct of the Artemision is a swamp. The ruins of the temple have sunk into the ground and vanished.

Not until 1863 was the site of the Artemision rediscovered, when in the course of his searches the English engineer Wood was finally guided to the right location by an inscription of Caius Vibius Salutarius found in the theatre at Ephesus concerning a gift of

The Artemision, rediscovered in 1869, as it is today

thirty-one gold and silver statues to the temple. Working for seven years, he brought to light an astonishing series of fragments, in particular segments of columns covered with reliefs, the *columnae caelatae*, or sculptured columns.

Carved on them were the stories of the gods and heroes. We see the return of Persephone, daughter of the goddess of the earth's produce, who was brought back from Hades in the underworld. Hermes, the messenger of the gods, accompanies her. Or Hercules making amends to Apollo for his crime, obliged to serve Queen Omphale for three years in woman's dress while she wore his lion-skin and carried his club. Or Theseus, the hero who vanquished Sinis, the giant and highwayman who would fasten his victims between two

Opposite: 'Angel of Death', detail from a sculptured column from the Hellenistic-age Artemision (British Museum, London)
Below: Fragment of the head of a boy, probably from the archaic temple of Artemis at Ephesus
Bottom: Detail from a fragment of a sculptured column (British Museum, London)
Overleaf: Scale model of the Artemision of Ephesus (British Museum, London)

pine trees he bent together and then let spring apart.

We see victory-gods leading bulls and sheep to the sacrifice, and Muses, the maidens created by Zeus, singing the heroes' praises and teaching men the arts of music and letters. Even these fragments, with their portraits of men and women and fateful battles of mythology, suffice to show how rich and magnificent the complete structure must have been.

On the basis of these finds, and subsequent excavations and surveys, supplemented with quotations and measurements from classical sources, it became possible to form a reconstructed picture of this World Wonder.

With only the classical authors to guide him, Fischer von Erlach had already attempted a portrayal of the

Below: Reconstructed ground-plan of the Artemision of
Ephesus
Bottom: General view of the site of the Artemision as it is today

Artemision in 1725. Later researches revealed that he
had been not at all far from the truth.

A major contribution to our present-day knowledge
has been made by the coins minted in the reign of the
emperor Hadrian during the second century AD, which
show both the Artemision and the goddess Artemis.
The ground-plan that has meanwhile been reconstructed gives a clear idea of the layout.

The cella housing the shrine and statue of Artemis
was surrounded by the temple itself, which measured
425 by 220 Greek feet – in modern terms, 413 by 214 feet.
The figure of 127 columns mentioned by Pliny is quite
possible, since there were nine columns across the back
of the temple and only eight across the westward-facing
front end.

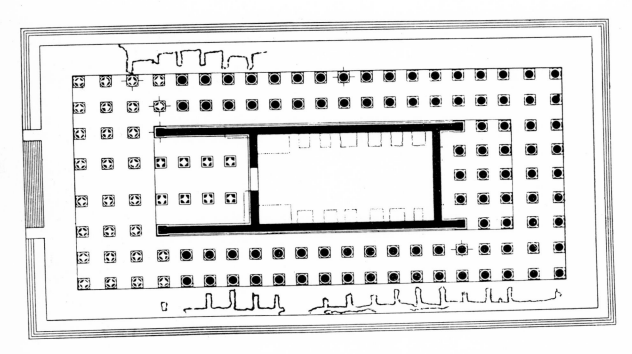

Of the 127 columns, thirty-six bore sculptured reliefs, and these were in all probability situated at the front end of the temple. The columns reached a height of almost sixty-five feet. Their radius at the base amounted to one-twelfth of the height. The remains of the temple of Apollo at Didyma, to the south of Miletus, which was begun at the same time as the Artemision (the same architects worked on sections of both buildings) give a very good indication of how the Artemision at Ephesus would have appeared.

The Ephesian Artemis, in contrast to all the Greek temple gods, looked from the east towards the west, from the sunrise towards the sunset, from Asia towards Europe.

She was goddess of the chaste day and mysterious

Below: Surviving capital from the Artemision (British Museum, London)
Bottom: The temple of Apollo at Didyma, seen from the east

ruler of the night, the keen huntress and mother of help-less dumb animals, the symbol of both child-like sim-plicity and imponderability, full of sweetness and charm with her entrancing smile and yet wild, cruel and implacable.

But she was also the goddess of wild and inviolable nature, the incarnation of the perceptive faculty of the male and the refined emotion of the female. She stood squarely facing her worshippers, straight and almost stiff, with her legs and feet firmly together. Her elbows were held at her sides, while her hands were extended outwards. Over a light tunic, the *chiton*, visible only at her feet and on her arms, she wore a solid, leather-like garment, the *ependytes*, which covered her legs and hips. It was decorated with reliefs of rams, lions, oxen, griffins, deer and bees. Across her front the goddess wore a device representing many-breastedness and symbolising the Great Mother. On the goddess's arms and shoulders were lions and mythical beasts.

The original temple-statue of Ephesus, made of gold, ebony, silver and black stone, has not survived. The many copies in stone, however, that have survived – mainly from imperial Rome – all show, despite variations, the same basic type for the Great Mother. The coins, too, give us clear pictures of the temple and its statue, and reveal to us an undestroyed and indestructible tradition.

While young men and fair-girdled girls flocked through the Coressus gate on the processional way, praying, singing and dancing as they moved towards

Opposite: Lower half of the statue of Artemis at Ephesus (pictured on p. 198) showing details of the relief on the *chiton* (Ephesus Museum)
Above: The bee, sacred to Artemis, from the statue shown on p. 198 and opposite
Right: Statue of Artemis from Roman times, found at Ephesus – on the head-piece is a representation of a temple (Ephesus Museum)

the sanctuary a mile away, and the goddess Artemis smiled down on the virgin priestesses as they danced and on the sacrifices set before her, away in his capital of Pasargardae in the uplands of Iran the great Cyrus was arming his troops – Cyrus, the King of Kings and commander of the Persian empire.

He defeated the invading army of King Croesus of Lydia in 546 BC at Pteria, and immediately ordered his troops to march westwards. The Persians took Sardis by storm, Croesus was made prisoner and, at Cyrus's command, condemned to be burnt on the pyre. According to the account in Herodotus, however, a kind stroke of fate saved him from the flames.

Ephesus and all the Greek cities on the west coast of Asia Minor came under Persian rule. Artemis of the

Below: The processional way and Coressus gate at Ephesus as they are today; the way led from the former harbour to the Artemision
Bottom: Head of a Lydian, claimed to be a portrait of King Croesus – painted terracotta miniature (Excavation house, Sardis)
Opposite: Male torso, found at Delphi (Delphi Museum)

Ephesians remained intact. She still gazed from the east towards the west, and still remained the mediatrix between Asia and Europe. Cyrus, whose rule extended from Ionia to Babylon, died in 529, mortally wounded in battle. His body was laid to rest in a monumental tomb at Pasargardae, the capital of Persia's newly-established world empire.

Kings came and went, for two centuries fighting men marched from east to west, battles were fought, cities were captured and then freed, alliances were formed and broken, men were born and died, kingdoms rose and fell, but the Greek people and their culture survived through it all. The goddess Artemis and her temple at Ephesus also endured, a refuge for the persecuted and the dispossessed, and her services and festivals remained.

Symposium with *hetaerae* (courtesans), painted on a bell-shaped bowl (Naples Museum)

But Ephesus was also a rich and pleasure-loving city. Men and women wore violet, purple and saffron-coloured dress, and cloaks in the hyacinth blue of Egypt, or of Persian cloth with grains of pure gold strewn over a scarlet background. They drank the sweet wine in abundance, and eagerly made love.

One night in the year 356, in a fit of madness, a man set a burning torch to the temple and statue of the goddess Artemis. The goddess fell, the roof cracked, and the columns toppled. The madman had started the fire for no more reason than to ensure his immortality by committing this monstrous act. The Ephesians, on pain of death, forbade the very mention of his name. In spite of this his name is known: Herostratus.

During that dreadful night a man was born who was

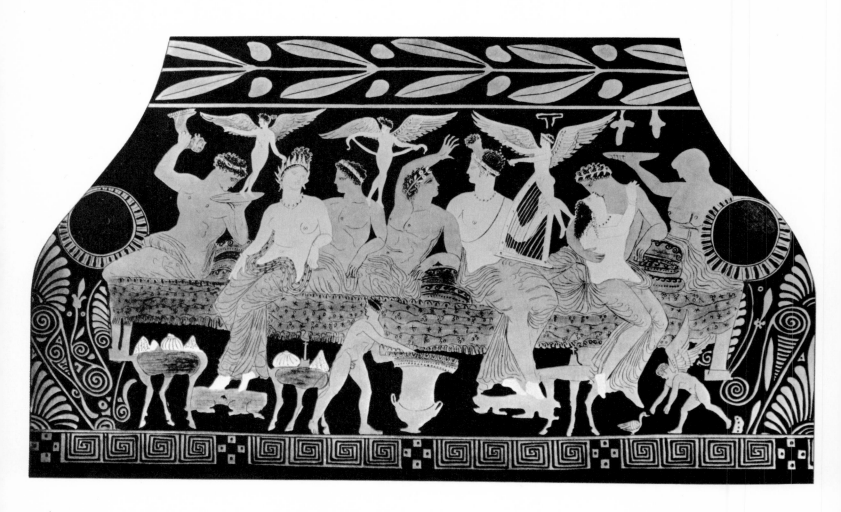

destined to shake the world: Alexander of Macedon, who even in his own lifetime was called the Great.

Twenty-two years later the young Alexander led forty thousand Macedonians and Greeks in a campaign of liberation against the Persians, advancing across the Hellespont to the River Granicus in Asia Minor, where, on the further bank, forty thousand men of the Persian army were waiting for him, including twenty thousand Greek mercenaries in battle array. Against the advice of his generals, Alexander, after spirited opposition from the Persians, forced his way across the river, completely defeated them along with the bravely fighting mercenaries, and only escaped a death-blow aimed by a Persian through the intervention of a friend.

He marched on to the strongly-garrisoned city of

Bust of Alexander the Great, found at Alexandria (British Museum, London)

Sardis, which he captured, and also entered Ephesus.

He wanted to expedite the rebuilding of the temple of Artemis. But the Ephesians replied: 'It is not fitting for a god to build the abode of a goddess.' Alexander paid homage to the goddess with a magnificent military parade and with festive games, and exempted the city from all taxes and tributes.

The people of Ephesus spent one hundred and twenty years building the new temple of Artemis, and finally completed the new building after the middle of the third century BC. This temple was held to be one of the Wonders of the World even in its own day. The new building followed the same ground-plan as its predecessor in every detail. Length, breadth, height, were completely identical. Wall stood over wall, column over

Below: View of the River Granicus, where the battle between the Macedonians and the Persians was fought in 334 BC
Opposite: The statue of the Ephesian Artemis compared with a modern Turkmen woman in festive costume

column, as though they had sprung up from common roots. Even the arrangement of the sculptured columns was the same.

The only difference was that this time the temple was built on a platform of thirteen steps, and consequently stood eight feet ten inches higher than the old one.

And the goddess once more gazed from the east out westwards: the mediatrix between Asia and Europe, the refuge of the dispossessed and persecuted, the Great Mother of the world. Fighting men marched once again, this time from west to east, once more battles were fought, alliances formed and betrayed.

Greece's power declined and Rome rose up. Caesar's star climbed and flickered out. The earth was steeped with men's blood. Then Octavian crushed the forces of

217

Mark Antony and his ally Cleopatra in the sea-battle at Actium. As the emperor Augustus he brought two centuries of peace to the Mediterranean world.

But above all the turmoil, above all the bloodshed and slaughter, the Artemis of Ephesus stood tall and strong. While the Roman emperors came and went, Ephesus grew more splendid and beautiful than ever.

When the apostle Paul came from Tarsus to Ephesus, and proclaimed in the theatre the doctrine of Christ who died on the cross, and preached against the Artemis of the Ephesians, he caused an uproar among the twenty-five thousand who filled the broad circle. 'Great is Artemis of the Ephesians!' the crowd shouted and stormed; 'Great is Artemis of the Ephesians!'

Paul was forced to leave the city before sunset. In the

Below left: Relief depicting the mother-goddess Cybele (Ephesus Museum)
Below right: Archaic statuette of the goddess Artemis, found at Ephesus (Istanbul Museum)
Opposite: Relief portraying the Virgin Mary, from about 800 AD, found at Ephesus (Ephesus Museum)

year 263 AD the temple of Artemis was barbarously plundered and destroyed by the Goths, who at that time were making pirate raids in the Aegean.

But the divine works in strange ways: the city where the Great Mother had ruled became the home of the mother of Jesus Christ, the Son of God.

St John the Evangelist, fulfilling the task entrusted to him by the crucified Christ, is said to have prepared a dwelling for Mary on the Bulbul Dag, the Nightingale or Coressus mountain.

Thus the image persisted of the Great Mother, the sustainer of men and beasts, the protectress of all creatures on earth, the virgin mother. Still the rich image of her dwelling-place persists, the Artemision of Ephesus, though all that survives today are a few fragments.

Fragment of a relief from the Roman period with the emblem 'A' (for Artemis); Artemis is shown on the left, with animals, while on the right is a priest (Ephesus Museum)

The Mausoleum at Halicarnassus

Mausolus was tyrant of Caria, the country situated on the south-west coast of Asia Minor, and he died in the fourth year of the 106th Olympiad – i.e., 353 BC. He and his tomb, known as the *Maussolleion*, or Mausoleum, and included among the Seven Wonders of the World, were described by the Roman Pliny the elder, who was a cavalry general in Germany, commander of the fleet under the emperor Vespasian, and an encyclopaedic author whose knowledge was acquired through his own observations and from two thousand books written by others. He reports:

'The Mausoleum measures thirty-six feet on the north and south sides, somewhat less across front and back, and in its total periphery measures 411 feet. It reaches a height of twenty-five cubits, and is surrounded by a

Below: Battle between Greeks and Amazons, from the frieze of the Mausoleum at Halicarnassus (British Museum, London)
Bottom: Battles between Greeks and Amazons, from the frieze of the Mausoleum (British Museum, London)
Opposite: Fragment from the so-called Amazon frieze that stood on the Mausoleum at Halicarnassus (British Museum, London)

peristyle of thirty-six columns, above which rises a twenty-four-step pyramid surmounted by a four-horse chariot made of marble.'

Caria, the rocky country to the south of the River Maeander in the south-west corner of Asia Minor, with its elaborate and deeply-indented coastline, protected to the rear by vast mountains, was an ideal territory for the bold, sea-going barbarians, the Carians, who dwelt there.

Darius of Persia, King of Kings, whom foreign cunning and his own courage had brought to the throne in the year 522 BC, included Caria among the countries on which he imposed tribute.

But two hundred years later Mausolus, tyrant of Halicarnassus and ruler of Caria since 377 BC, scarcely took

A stairway in the theatre at Miletus

his title of satrap, or Persian provincial governor, seriously any longer. He did whatever he saw fit. In the year 374 BC he took part in the revolt in which all the subject nations of the coastal satrapies, who had allied themselves with Egypt, rose up against the Persians under Artaxerxes II. A year later he accompanied the same Persian monarch on a punitive expedition against the Egyptians. He was an unscrupulous as well as an independent ruler.

Next, on his own initiative, he made war on the powerful and beautiful city of Miletus, with its four harbours on the mouth of the Maeander. He also led a campaign against the wealthy city of Ephesus, which commanded an area extending far out to the west. He subjugated the freedom-loving Greeks of Ionia, on the

coast between Aeolia and Caria, and a part of Lydia, the land to the north of Caria. He also imposed tribute on Lycia, rich in precious woods and fine wines.

He controlled all the offshore islands along the Carian coast, and contrived to incite the shrewd and powerful islanders of Rhodes, Cos and Chios to break away from Athens in the Social War (357–355 BC). He tricked the Lycians into paying a poll-tax by telling them that the Persian king had issued an order stating that all their hair must be yielded up to make wigs for Persian ladies and gentlemen, but that he would prevent this by levying a cash payment for the Persians and exerting his own powerful influence.

He extracted a large sum of money from the citizens of Mylasa, his first capital, by promising a new wall to

Below: The winding Maeander river as it approaches the sea, seen from the acropolis of Miletus
Bottom: Fragments of the so-called Eros frieze in the theatre at Miletus

protect the city against its enemies. But when the Mylasians reminded him about the defensive wall, he told them that the gods had forbidden him to build it.

With the money he built his new capital, Halicarnassus – a palace and fortress combined – on a steep rock sloping down to the Ceramic gulf. He added a secret naval station, screened by the island of Arconnesus, which enabled him to mobilise his fleet unobserved by enemy eyes.

He was married – as was the custom in Egypt also – to his sister, Artemisia, who idolised her brother and husband and fully matched him in boldness and cunning.

Mausolus died in 353 after a reign lasting twenty-four years. His wife and sister Artemisia assumed control of

Below: Remains of a city gate and defensive walls dating from the time of King Mausolus at Halicarnassus
Bottom: Road leading from the ancient city of Halicarnassus, still in use today
Opposite: View of the harbour at Bodrum (Halicarnassus); the light patches in the water are the foundations of the ancient harbour

Caria until her death. She summoned to Halicarnassus the most famous Greek architects, headed by Pythius, and the most gifted sculptors, led by the great Scopas, in order to build a tomb for the dead tyrant such as the world had never seen before. Mausolus had had thoughts of his own self-glorification while he still lived, and had made preparations for it.

At the same time the fleet under Artemisia's command set sail for Rhodes, and the Carians brought the people, city and port under subjection, displaying both cruelty and cunning. Artemisia died in 351 BC before the Mausoleum was fully completed. But, as Pliny relates, the artists she had commissioned continued working on the World Wonder 'for love', and it was finished that same year.

Below left: Colossal statue of Artemisia which probably surmounted the Mausoleum at Halicarnassus along with the statue of her brother Mausolus (British Museum, London)
Bottom: Fragment of the head of Artemisia, belonging to the statue on the left (British Museum, London)
Opposite: Colossal statue of King Mausolus, probably by the Greek sculptor Bryaxis; the fragments from which it was pieced together were found on the north side of the Mausoleum

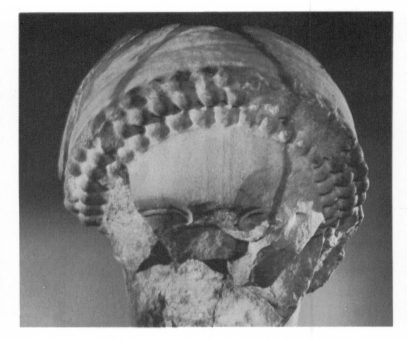

Opposite: Head of one of the horses from the chariot that surmounted the Mausoleum together with the figures of Mausolus and his sister (British Museum, London)
Below: Reconstruction of the Mausoleum's appearance, by Professor Fritz Krischen

Eighteen years later, Alexander the Great marched into Caria to great popular acclaim as the 'liberator from Persian rule'. The city and fortress of Halicarnassus, which the Persians continued to defend for some considerable time, was razed to the ground after Alexander's decisive victory. Caria's history was thus brought to a close.

As a Roman province, Caria enjoyed one final release from obscurity. The Mausoleum remained untouched by all the upheavals. Philo of Byzantium quotes fourth-century BC authors whose accounts indicate that it was well preserved. And such reports persisted as late as the twelfth century.

The period when the Mausoleum began to fall into ruin cannot be established. It is probable that first of

all an earthquake brought down the upper part of the monument. The Frenchman Claude Guichard states in 1581 that the Knights of the Order of St John 'destroyed one of the Seven Wonders of the World that had survived all the barbarian onslaughts'. The Knights of the Order of St John, defenders of the Holy Land and zealous opponents of the Turks, fled before their enemies to Rhodes, where they could muster a powerful fleet and continue their battle against the infidels. In 1402 they took possession of Halicarnassus to use as a naval station, and built the fortress of St Peter at the harbour entrance. In doing so they used all the ruins of the Mausoleum that lay round about. In the course of a hundred years they systematically extended the fortifications, using the World Wonder throughout as a

Below: The fortress of St Peter overlooking the harbour at Halicarnassus; it was built in 1402 by the Knights of St John from the stones of the Mausoleum
Bottom: Sculptured lion from the Mausoleum, incorporated in the walls of the fortress of St Peter
Opposite: Sculptured lion from the Mausoleum, built into the 'English tower' of the fortress of St Peter

PROPTER CATHOLIC

Opposite: Detail from the Amazon frieze of the Mausoleum of
Halicarnassus (British Museum, London)
Below: Part of the Amazon frieze of the Mausoleum; on the
left is an Amazon mounted in reverse (British Museum, London)
Bottom: Recently-discovered fragment of the Amazon frieze,
found in the courtyard of the St Peter fort

stone-quarry. They tore down all that would come down, and carried away whatever they could. Such treasures as were hidden away were later carried off by the corsairs.

When Fischer von Erlach illustrated the Mausoleum in his *Entwurff einer Historischen Architectur* ('Outline for a Historical Architecture'), he had nothing but the classical sources to guide him.

All that remained undestroyed by the Knights of St John were thirteen carved panels depicting Amazons in battle, which they had built into the walls of the fortress. European visitors were admiring them from the middle of the seventeenth century, without anyone at the time knowing where the panels originated. But finally the view was propounded that these reliefs must have

239

belonged to the frieze on the outside of the Mausoleum. Descriptions and drawings of them began to appear. Towards the middle of the nineteenth century, the desire to save these unique works of art from destruction grew so strong in Europe that the British Ambassador in Constantinople, Stratford Canning, requested the Sultan's permission for the reliefs to be removed from the fortress. The Sultan granted the request, and presented the sculptures as a gift to the British Museum in London, where they are still cared for today as one of the treasures of the world.

However, this did not help to solve the puzzle regarding the site, ground-plan and appearance of the Mausoleum. When the English scholar Sir Charles Newton made a first journey to Halicarnassus in 1853, a

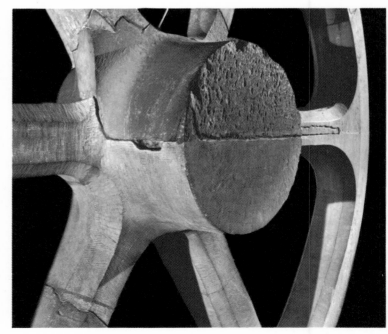

Capital of one of the columns that supported the pyramid-shaped roof of the Mausoleum (British Museum, London)

new phase began in the exploration of this World Wonder. In the walls of the fortress Newton discovered lions' heads of which the material and artistry indicated beyond doubt that they came from the Mausoleum. These discoveries led the British government to equip an expedition and send it to Halicarnassus.

The detailed descriptions given by the Roman architect Vitruvius, who not only carried out major commissions for Caesar and Augustus, but was also an important author and wrote on the principles and history of architecture, led to the discovery of the platform on which the Mausoleum had stood. Between the agora and the temple of Ares was where the researchers were finally able to locate it.

The world greeted the resulting discoveries with

amazement – in particular the statue of Mausolus himself, successfully pieced together from sixty-three fragments, and that of his sister, along with lions and lions' heads, bases of columns and one complete column, fragments of a horse, a huge stone chariot wheel and the heads of various male figures.

Probably every one of these sculptures and architectural details comes from the upper part of the Mausoleum. They were brought down by an earthquake, disappeared beneath the surface, and so escaped the enthusiastic building operations of the Knights.

In addition to these, an alabaster vase was discovered inscribed in Persian, Babylonian and Egyptian with the name of Xerxes, the Great King of Persia. But the detailed appearance of the World Wonder remained a

Below: Fragment of a male head found at the site of the Mausoleum and doubtless once a part of it (British Museum, London)
Overleaf: General view of the remains of the mausoleum at Belevi, ten miles north-east of Ephesus

matter for theory and speculation among individual researchers. The main question which arose, and still arises, was this: was the Mausoleum the first and only building of its kind?

Situated on the west coast of Asia Minor, Halicarnassus was, geographically and historically, a meeting point for the cultures of east and west. Here the art and history of Mesopotamia and Persia bordered on that of Athens and Greece. The military campaigns of the Persians and the rule of their kings and satraps inevitably left their mark.

The Tower of Babel, shrine of the god of the heavens, afterwards also called the tomb of Baal-Belos, which rose up in a series of gradually diminishing stages, provided the inspiration and model for the tomb of the

Great King of Persia, Cyrus II, in Pasargardae. Set on a high pedestal, it resembles a religious building – temple, tomb and dwelling-place all in one: the dead king has become a god. This was the western version of the towers of the eastern nations.

It is probably right to regard Mausolus as a minor dynastic ruler within the Persian world empire who nevertheless had sufficient power and money to emulate the tomb of the great Cyrus and even try to outmatch it. With the help of the most important artists of his time, Mausolus produced a classical Greek version of the royal tomb of the Persians, and it appears that he in turn had successors who imitated his building. The ruins of a tomb near the present-day village of Belevi, nine miles north-east of Ephesus, provide a most interesting

The mausoleum at Milas

parallel to the Mausoleum of Halicarnassus. In the actual rock of a tall hill sloping down to the plain of the Cayster, a block was carved out measuring fifty feet in height and eighty-two feet along each side, and lined with heavy ashlar marble. On a platform of three steps stood a square-shaped cella with a great many reliefs set into its outside walls. Only portions of these have survived, depicting battles between men and Centaurs. The cella was surrounded by slender Corinthian columns. Above this peristyle rose the roof-pyramid, which had winged lions at each corner of its cornice.

The tomb chamber is located in the south side of the supporting structure. It was hewn out of the rock and lined with ashlar marble in the form of barrel-vaults. Here the sarcophagus still stood until quite recently,

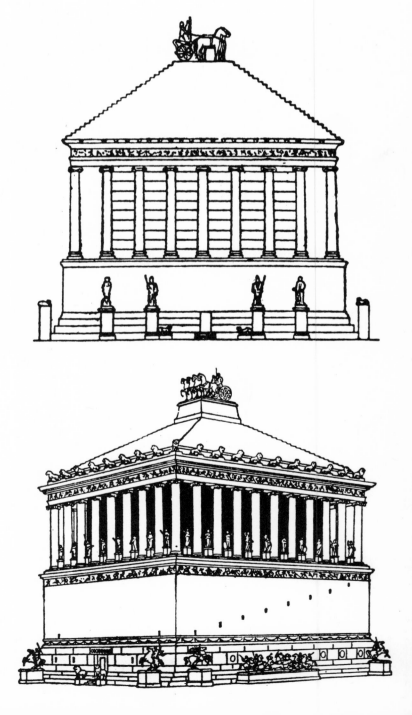

resembling a bed, with the sculptured figure of the dead man lying on it – a 'lord'. We do not know his name or who he was. Perhaps a satrap to the King of Kings who fell when the young Alexander made his march along the west coast of Asia Minor . . .

This mausoleum at Belevi, which for many centuries was unknown, provides a mysterious reflection of the larger one at Halicarnassus.

Today we are able to reconstruct the appearance of the Mausoleum with reasonable certainty. It reached a total height of 115 feet. The foundations, embedded in the rock, formed a rectangle 127 feet long by 108 feet wide. On this was a platform with six steps, and above it, reaching a considerable height, was the lower stage of the building, which formed the actual support and provided space for two friezes set one above the other,

Left: Greek warrior – detail from the Amazon frieze which decorated the Mausoleum at Halicarnassus (British Museum, London)
Opposite: Alabaster vase for precious ointments, inscribed in Persian, Babylonian and Egyptian with the name of King Xerxes of Persia; it was probably a gift from the king to Artemisia, about 480 BC – found on the site of the Mausoleum at Halicarnassus (British Museum, London)

while a third frieze lined the walls of the cella above. On top of this supporting structure were thirty-six Ionic columns, forming a row of nine along the shorter sides and eleven along the longer sides. They surrounded the cella, which was probably guarded by lions placed between the columns.

Resting on the columns and the architrave that surmounted them was the twenty-four-step roof-pyramid, with gargoyles in the form of lions' heads spaced regularly along it. The roof-pyramid was left flat at the top, thus providing a platform for the crowning feature, a marble quadriga with four life-size horses and a chariot in which stood the figures of Mausolus and Artemisia.

The building followed the law of the Golden Section, and the individual elements were combined according

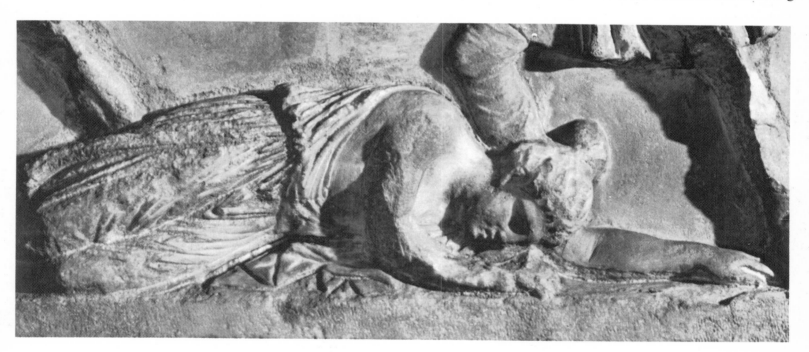

to the proportions provided by this law. The same arrangement of Ionic columns and entablature was found in the temple of Athena at Priene, which was also built by Pythius.

This is the probable meaning of the Mausoleum of Halicarnassus:

The lord and sovereign is laid to rest in the vicinity of heaven, above the conflict between cosmos and chaos, order and confusion, nature and the unnatural, that is portrayed on the surrounding friezes. There are no steps or paths leading up to where he lies.

Thus he will never return, the mortal who has been elevated to the gods, enthroned above land and sea.

He is beyond reach, his reputation is beyond reach, even though his body has crumbled away to dust.

One of the lions'-heads that served as water-spouts on the roof of the Mausoleum at Halicarnassus (British Museum, London)

The Colossus of Rhodes

Rhodes, the island lying off the coast of Caria, is the special province of Helios, the god of light, who can see everything that happens on earth. A bronze statue of him stood on the island, and it was so vast that it was included as the 'Colossus of Rhodes' among the Seven Wonders of the World.

Pindar, the poet of Thebes, relates in his seventh Olympian Ode:

'And the tale is told in ancient story, when Zeus and the immortals were dividing up the earth among them, Rhodes was not yet to be seen in the billowing sea, for it was hidden in the briny deeps. Because he was absent, no-one allotted Helios his due portion. Thus it happened that the blameless god was left with no land of his own. He called attention to this, and Zeus wanted to cast

Left: View of the coast of Rhodes from the top of the acropolis at Lindus
Opposite: Head of the sun-god Helios – Rhodian sculpture probably dating from about 200 BC (Rhodes Museum)

fresh lots. But Helios would not allow it. For within the foaming sea, he said, his eyes could see a plot of land rising up from the bottom, rich in substance for many men and kindly for pasture. And straight away he made the goddess of fate swear on the golden snood, and Zeus nodded his consent, that the island risen into the realm of light should be his ever after.'

We are told the race of Telchines emerged from the depths of the sea with the island, metal-workers and magicians who tricked the gods with their magic arts until Apollo, the far-striker, slew them with his arrows.

Whereupon Helios took over the island – the youth with 'shining eyes and golden locks', brother of the goddesses and the moon and the dawn, who each morning in the far east near Colchis mounted a chariot drawn by

four fiery steeds, steered his regular circle across the sky, and in the evening plunged into the Ocean stream in the far west, returning during the night to the far east.

On the island, beside the murmuring streams, he celebrated his marriage with Rhode, the shy nymph of the race of naiads. And the dryads, the lovely sisters of Rhode, made the trees tremble in the groves with their sweet song. The nymph Rhode bore the god sons named Camirus, Ialysus and Lindus. Their father's realm was divided into three, and each then dwelt separately in a city of his own that bore his name:

White Camirus, the most powerful of the three cities, lay on the west of the island, and was surmounted by the temple of Pallas Athene, the daughter of Zeus, in whom warlike strength was combined with shining wisdom.

Below: Avenue leading to the sea near Ialysus, Rhodes
Overleaf: Ruins of the city of Camirus, seen from the cistern

Below: Terracotta head of Athena (Istanbul Museum)
Opposite below: Road through Camirus, leading to the acropolis from the sea
Opposite bottom: Semicircular bench for the judges in the agora at Camirus

Ialysus, the city on the north-west tip of the island, was also dedicated to Athena. The acropolis, a fortress and temple combined, stood on Mount Philerimus, beneath which spread fields and woods filled with the chirping of thousands of crickets and the flight of countless butterflies. The descendants of the first inhabitants buried their dead round the tomb of Ialysus on three hills which rose in front of the acropolis, overlooking the sea to which they owed the birth of their island.

Lindus, the city belonging to Helios's third son, commanded the east coast of the island. Like its sister-cities, this too was protected by Athena, the goddess of ships, of which there is one carved in relief on the cliffs.

Cleobulus, a subsequent ruler at Lindus and one of

the Seven Wise Men of Greece, had his tomb built on a small volcanic island opposite Athena's sanctuary.

Tlepolemus, the son of Hercules, obliged by fate to slay his uncle, sailed to Rhodes with a large following as a fugitive from Argos in the east of the Peloponnese. They divided into three tribes and dwelt in the cities of Camirus, Ialysus and Lindus. The Heraclid ruled over them all, a great, powerful and peaceful reign. Rhodian trade and shipping flourished under Helios's protection.

But when Eris, the goddess of strife, threw down the apple inscribed 'For the Fairest' into the assembly of the immortals on Olympus, the mountain of the gods, the resulting conflict was implanted by the gods on earth. Paris, the son of the aged Priam of Troy, eloped with the beautiful Helen, wife of King Menelaus of Sparta.

Agamemnon, king of Mycenae and the bravest of the Greek princes, led the Greek army against Troy, and the Trojan war 'that provoked unspeakable misery' began. The Heraclid Tlepolemus also sailed to Troy, with nine ships and 'the defiant youths of Rhodes', and was there slain by Sarpedon, the king of Lycia, a son of Zeus.

To Rhodes, now without a ruler, came Althaemenes of Crete, after an oracle had made him fear that he might kill his father Catreus. He was followed by members of the brave race of Dorians, who established a colony.

When Catreus came to Rhodes as an old man to pass on the Cretan throne to his son, he was nevertheless slain unrecognised by Althaemenes in a fight.

The cities of Camirus, Ialysus and Lindus, peacefully

growing more and more prosperous, allied themselves with the island cities of Cnidus and Cos and with Halicarnassus on the mainland to form the Dorian Hexapolis, the League of Six Cities.

Diagoras, the political leader of Rhodes in the fifth century BC, one of the greatest of all Greek athletes, chief contestant and victor at all four major festivals of sacred games, and celebrated in verse by his contemporary Pindar, led Rhodes on the side of Athens in the struggle against the Persians. But Pindar probably had a reason for closing his seventh Olympian Ode, which dealt with Diagoras, with the words: 'Straight is his path, that hates insolence. The Eratids celebrate his victory, the city celebrates it also. But, in a moment, the winds blow differently from day to day.'

Relief of a Greek ship, carved in the cliffs at Lindus

Doreus, Diagoras's son and successor, himself a champion athlete, who suppressed a popular uprising in 411 BC, met with varying degrees of favour from his contemporaries. But this bold and far-sighted ruler successfully founded the city of Rhodes around a fine new harbour on the north-east tip of the island, attracted to it the best people from the old cities of Camirus, Ialysus and Lindus, and made the four cities strong and ready to defend themselves. In this way he was able to safeguard the island's power and wealth against enemy attack, and under his rule Rhodes reached a new level of prosperity.

On the highest point of the island a temple was built to Zeus, the shepherd of the peoples. But his son Apollo was also honoured. They built a temple like a citadel to

the Delphic god who had taught the Greeks that a well-timed sacrifice would rob even the most powerful enemy of his weapons of destruction.

But the times did not favour such hopes. The course of Rhodian history during the seventy-five years that followed the founding of the temple up until the time of Alexander the Great's world empire was dictated by the conflicts between Athens and Sparta, the battles between Greeks and Persians, and the civil wars between the aristocratic families and the people of Rhodes.

When Alexander was preparing the ground for his campaign against Persia, Rhodes was made to receive a Macedonian garrison, and thus lost its independence.

Following Alexander's death in 323 BC, the island's freedom under the sign of its ruling god was restored. In

Head of a man of Rhodes – archaic sculpture of about 600 BC (Istanbul Museum)

271

those years, Rhodes reached the height of its power.

The city's harbour became the most important shipping centre for grain, pitch, building timber, skins, hemp, woollen goods and slaves. As a result of Alexander's generalship and political activities, the Hellenic world became one enormous market, dominated by Greek merchants. Prices were determined by the money of the great trading powers, and credit and banking establishments exerted a growing influence on politics.

But Alexander was dead. And since there was no heir of full age, his generals split the world empire up into separate kingdoms and set themselves up as their rulers. Thus the one-eyed Antigonus, one of Alexander's most capable generals, successfully competed for control of Macedonia and Greece.

Below: Dying warrior – sculpture from the east pediment of the temple of Aphaea at Aegina (Glyptothek, Munich)
Opposite: Head of a *kore* (maiden) of Lindus, about 200 BC (Istanbul Museum)

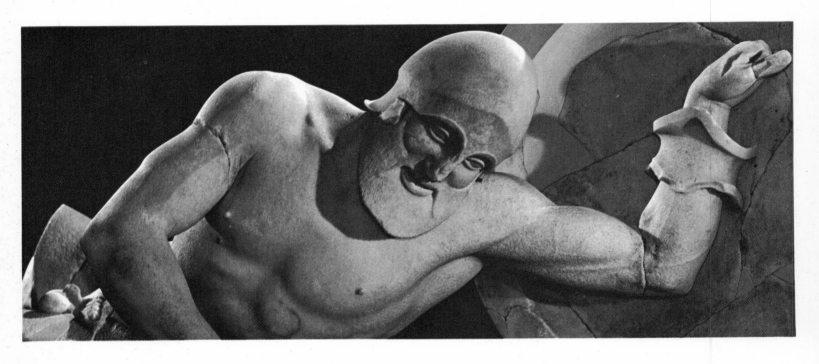

When, in the year 304, he sent his son Demetrius Poliorcetes, the destroyer of cities – who had grown up in the camps of Alexander – against Rhodes with a fleet of warships, the island kingdom faced its darkest hour. Demetrius had a special weapon: large ships fitted with siege engines of his own construction. They became the terror of his enemies. But the Rhodians defended their city courageously, and Demetrius was obliged to call off the siege and leave many dead – and the costly war engines – behind.

But man can do nothing without the gods; the Rhodians realised this. Therefore they wanted to build a statue of the god Helios, the lord and protector of their island, and they decided to finance one from the proceeds of the war engines.

Below: The harbour of the city of Rhodes, showing the Fort St Nicholas
Bottom: Fragment of a stone sundial in the theatre at Rhodes
Opposite: Bronze statue of a youth from Trabzon (Istanbul Museum)

Opposite: Relief of Helios (fragment) found at Rhodes, probably portraying the Colossus itself (Rhodes Museum)
Below left: Reconstruction of the Colossus of Rhodes by the British archaeologist Herbert Maryon
Below right: Reconstruction of the Colossus of Rhodes by Fischer von Erlach (British Museum Library, London)

The Greek geographer Strabo, who travelled the world to its farthest accessible limits at about the time of the birth of Christ, relates:

'But the finest of all the votive gifts and statues in the city of Rhodes is the Colossus of Helios, which is said in the poem to have been built "seven times ten cubits high by Chares of Lindus". Now it lies on the ground, overthrown by an earthquake, severed at the knees.'

It is not certain where the Colossus of Helios stood; the classical sources reveal nothing on this point. A raised open space in the very centre of the ancient city is supposed by many researchers to have been its location, but they can offer no evidence. It is likely that a colossal statue of about one hundred feet in height would have stood at a point where it could be seen from a distance by

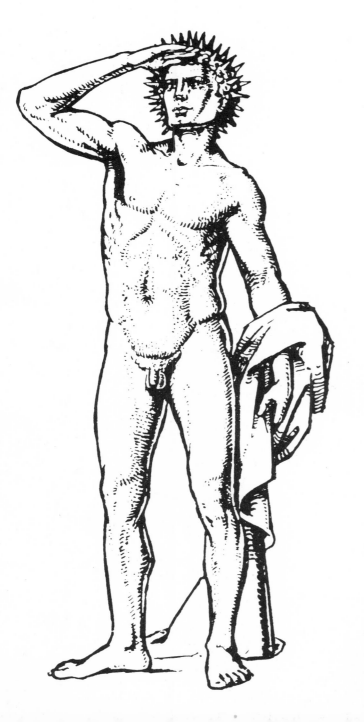

approaching ships and used as a landmark by the garrisons. Therefore it could well have stood precisely where the Fort St Nicholas is situated today, the outermost bastion of the fortifications built by the crusaders of the Order of St John in their fight against the Turks. A great deal of ancient remains were used in building the fort, and they can still be found today.

An engraving by Fischer von Erlach in 1725 shows the popular conception of the statue's stance and appearance that emerged during the Renaissance and which remains in many people's minds to this day: holding aloft a burning torch, Helios straddles the harbour entrance in such a way that ships in full sail can pass beneath him and enter the safety of the harbour. One foot must have rested on a platform on

Below: Man standing on the prow of a ship – from the burial stele of Demetrius, second half of the fourth century BC (British Museum, London)
Opposite: Bronze relief on the shoulder of a piece of armour depicting a battle between a Greek and an Amazon, dating from about 400–350 BC (British Museum, London)

Gold stater (standard coin) of 380–340 BC, from Rhodes. The obverse (left) shows the head of Helios, turned somewhat towards the right, with his hair streaming outwards to resemble the sun's rays; the picture is probably based on the Colossus of Rhodes. The reverse (right) shows a rose, the emblem of the island of Rhodes. (British Museum, London)

the left-hand end of the mole, and the other on the right-hand mole opposite. This charming conception is, however, not possible in practice, since the gap between the mole-like spits of land that form the natural harbours of Rhodes is too wide. In the case of the northern harbour, known today as the Mandraki port, the distance involved is over two hundred yards, and in the south harbour, the Commercial port, it is three hundred yards. The figure of one hundred feet given throughout the classical sources for the total height of the Colossus makes it highly doubtful whether seagoing craft ever passed beneath it. The statue would have needed to be considerably taller. Apart from being impossible technically, such a statue would have contradicted all the aesthetic principles of the Greeks of

the third century BC. This is another reason why we must abandon the romantic picture of Helios straddling the harbour walls – even though a business-minded tourist office plans to re-erect the statue of Helios on these lines.

When a stone relief of Helios was found at Rhodes in 1932, the Englishman Herbert Maryon undertook a new attempt at reconstructing its appearance. The relief, of which only the upper portion survives, undoubtedly portrays Helios, who is shading his eyes with his right hand and looking towards the right into the distance. Across his left arm lie the folds of his cloak, still just clearly recognisable as such. Because his head is turned sharply to one side, the trunk is also turned accordingly, a pose which is not found in the classical period of Greek

sculpture, but which becomes quite possible in Greek art after the time of the great sculptor Lysippus – in other words, the period which produced the statue of Helios.

The creator of the 'Colossus of Rhodes', however, was the sculptor Chares, a pupil of Lysippus.

A good parallel to it is provided by a sculpture of this period portraying the young Hercules, the work of the school of Lysippus, and by a bronze of the same school, showing one of the Diadochi, in which the non-supporting leg alters the rhythm of the body by being set back. And the statue of Marsyas playing the flute, where the figure is turned sharply about its own axis, provides a further comparison.

Despite severe weathering, the head of Helios in the

relief bears such a strong resemblance to another head of Helios which was likewise found at Rhodes that – when these are in turn compared with the head of Helius featured on Rhodian coins – a common link between them and the Colossus can safely be assumed.

Herbert Maryon bases his researches on the following facts derived from Philo of Byzantium: 'The Colossus was 120 feet high, and the materials used amounted to 12½ tons of bronze and 7½ tons of iron.' By calculating the relationship of the surface area to the amount of material used, Maryon was able to establish that the bronze shell could only have been 0.06 inches thick. He concludes from this that the separate sections from which the Colossus was assembled were not cast, as previously supposed, but hammered out. The figure's

Helios with the horses of the sun – metope from the temple of Athena at Ilium (Museum for Prehistory, Berlin)

stability, Maryon believes, depended entirely on what was inside it. This assertion accords not only with the description in Philo of Byzantium, but also with the information provided by Pliny in the *Naturalis Historia* after the fall of the Colossus: '. . . great cavities gape in the broken limbs, and inside them one can see stones of great size, which were used by the master to weigh the Colossus down.'

Maryon assumes that, partly to raise the Colossus above the level of the surrounding houses and hills and partly to enhance its aesthetic effect, it was placed on a pedestal some twenty feet high.

Philo and Strabo, who saw the Colossus at first hand after its collapse in an earthquake, refer to a massive framework of iron and stones within the figure. Maryon

Left: Rhodian woman in mourning – fragment of an Attic tomb relief of the third quarter of the fourth century BC (Glyptothek, Munich)
Opposite: Horses in geometrical style (height: 5.3 inches) from the lid of a circular casket of the middle of the eighth century BC (Glyptothek, Munich)

believes the framework to have consisted of two columns approximately ninety feet high running from the ankles through the legs and body up to the neck, and a third column some ten feet further away which passed through the drapery of the cloak that hung down to the ground from the left arm. Since there were no pulley-blocks or other lifting gear at that time, a mound must have been heaped up around the Colossus – a fact which also emerges from the account given by Philo of Byzantium. Materials for the statue were transported up a spiral ramp, and the mound was gradually built up as the statue gained height.

The figure is supposed to have taken twelve years to complete. Thus the Colossus grew up by an average of some ten feet a year. If one takes the raising of Deme-

Opposite: Steps and portico on the acropolis at Lindus
Right: Clay vase with animal friezes, found on the island of Rhodes (Rhodes Museum)

trius Poliorcetes' siege as the date when work began, then the Colossus must have been finished by about 290 BC.

But only sixty-six years later a terrible earthquake toppled the Colossus and at the same time destroyed parts of the walls and harbour of Rhodes. Twenty-five years afterwards, Rhodes' power and independence also collapsed.

In the year 653 AD the Saracen invaders of Rhodes tore down the remains of the World Wonder, stole the bronze, and carried it off to Syria.

There a merchant is said to have bought the bronze shell of the god and carried it away on nine hundred camels to be melted down.

Model of a Greek trireme (German Museum, Munich)

The Pharos of Alexandria

Opposite below: Scale model of the Pharos of Alexandria, built by Nagib Fanous according to the reconstructions of H. Thiersch (Qait Bay Fort, Alexandria)

Opposite bottom left: The Pharos with a ship – reverse of a coin (188–9 AD) from the time of the emperor Commodus (British Museum, London)

Opposite bottom right: The Pharos with the goddess Isis – reverse of a coin (148–9 AD) from the time of the emperor Antoninus Pius (British Museum, London)

Below: The Pharos, detail from a coin struck in 126–7 AD during the reign of the emperor Hadrian (Bodemuseum, Berlin)

The lighthouse which stood on the island of Pharos in the harbour of Alexandria was completed in the year 279 BC after twenty years' work. Almost from the first day it ranked as one of the Wonders of the World. Ptolemy II, king of Egypt, took advantage of its completion to celebrate amid great pomp the first pan-Hellenic national festival around a marvel of technical achievement. In modern terms, the building cost over £350,000 ($840,000) to produce.

At this time the Celts were invading Greece, and Rome and Carthage were concluding their alliance in order to destroy the Greeks in southern Italy. Epicurus was expounding unnoticed the theory that the world consisted of colliding atoms. And the beam of the lighthouse circled round, guiding ships and pointing the

way through a new age – an age that had begun 152 years before.

Athena, the shrewd daughter of Zeus, the protectress of all Greek cities and 'this land so wonderfully rich in glory, in warlike prowess, in poetry, in every strength', inclined her head in sorrow when the citizens of Athens and Sparta began in 431 BC to tear their own country to pieces in their struggle to win ascendancy over Greece. During the thirty years in which the young men were dying on the battlefields of the Peloponnesian War, the time was growing ripe for the Macedonians under King Philip II, who came to the throne in 359, to become the true masters of Greece.

On 4 August 338, the Macedonians stood face to face with the combined army of the Athenians and Thebans

Opposite: Musing Athena – dedicatory relief from the Acropolis, about 460 BC (Acropolis Museum, Athens)
Right: Lamenting woman – detail from the burial stele of Mnesarete, daughter of Socrates; Attic, about 380 BC (Glyptothek, Munich)

Opposite: An ephebe of Marathon – bronze statue of the fourth century BC (National Museum, Athens)
Below right: Thracian warriors – detail from a colossal tomb relief, about 100 AD, found at Salonika (Istanbul Museum)

on the plain of Chaeronea. King Philip evolved a completely new battle tactic: he opened the fighting with a manoeuvre by the light cavalry, in order to confuse his adversary, and sent in the infantry on a broad front to tie the enemy down while he carried out the operations on both flanks which decided the battle. The issue at Chaeronea was decided by a cavalry charge led by the young prince Alexander.

The victory memorial on the battlefield, a colossal lion made of marble, became the symbol of the pan-Hellenic league under the leadership of the Macedonians. Athens conferred honorary citizenship on the victorious Philip and his son Alexander, and the 'council of the Greeks' at Corinth assigned him absolute command in the war against Persia.

The lion monument at Chaeronea, in memory of the Macedonians who fell in the battle here in 338 BC

But the real victors were the gods of Greece and their priests and priestesses at Olympia, Delphi, Delos and Eleusis. It was the triumph of Homer, the poet of the *Iliad* and the *Odyssey*, who created a Greek language rich in imagery and suited equally to lyrical and dramatic expression; and of the great dramatist Aeschylus, who fought against the invaders from the east and then wrote the *Persians*; Sophocles, who in *Antigone* showed the conflict between law and the dictates of conscience; and Euripides, the author of *Medea, Phaedra* and *Iphigenia*.

The philosophers had triumphed: Socrates, who in his life and his teachings was the model of piety, self-control, fidelity to friends and convictions, patriotism and strength of character; Plato, the pupil of Socrates,

who saw the nature and meaning of the innate ideas of the human soul; and Theophrastus, father and founder of the science of plants and medicine. The emotions were charted by Sappho, the poetess who explored all the sweetness and sorrow of human existence, and by Alcaeus, the poet of angry passion and masculine strength. Aristotle, Plato's pupil, who taught Philip's young son Alexander and made him the greatest of all Greeks, was the thinker who summed up the age.

Aeschines, a pupil of Socrates and an eloquent public speaker at Athens, held the opinion that Asia could be conquered by a united Greece. When Alexander assumed power (336 BC) at the age of 22 in place of his father, who had been killed by his jealous wife, he consolidated his position in Macedonia and Greece

The battlefield at Chaeronea

299

and two years later began his war of vengeance against Persia.

He vanquished the strong city of Halicarnassus with its dangerous harbour, advanced into Gordium and made the highly significant gesture of releasing the Gordian Knot, on which, according to an ancient oracle, the fate of Asia hung, by cutting it through with his sword. He forestalled the Persian army that was advancing along the overland route by occupying the most important passes, and in 333 crushed the great Persian army under King Darius III at Issus. Darius fled.

Alexander brought Palestine under subjection and entered Egypt, where the population hailed him as their liberator from the Persian yoke. In 332 he founded the

city of Alexandria on the ridge of land between the Mediterranean and Lake Mareotis, and so established Greek power in Egypt. Then he travelled across the Libyan Desert to the famous oracle of Zeus in the Siwa oasis, and was declared by the priests to be the son of Zeus.

Now he marched as a god into Asia, and in the year 331 fought the decisive battle against the Persians on the plain between Arbela and Gaugamela in Assyria. King Darius was killed by his own officers. This victory made Alexander master of Asia.

At Persepolis he set fire to the palace of Xerxes in symbolic retaliation for the burning of Athens a hundred and fifty years earlier. With this, the war of vengeance against Persia was brought to a close.

Head of Plato, found at Ephesus (Ephesus Museum)

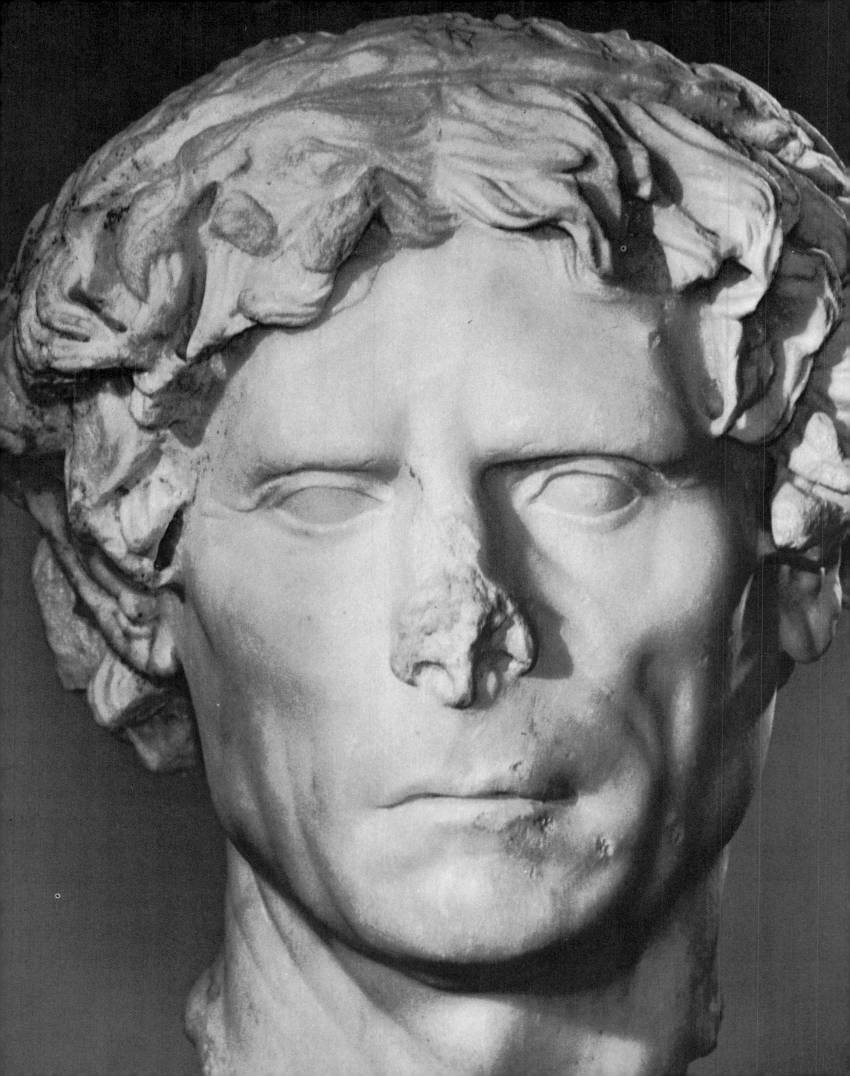

Opposite: Head of a priest, Hellenistic age (National Museum, Athens)

Right: Colossal head of King Ptolemy II of Egypt; he wears the crown of Egypt over Greek-style hair (Greco-Roman Museum, Alexandria)

After the march he made through India, Alexander returned to the Persian city of Susa in the year 324. He ordered peace celebrations to be held at Opis on the Tigris, and prayed for a peace in which Macedonians, Persians, Greeks and the people of all nations would be equal members of a single community, prayed that all the peoples of the world that he knew might live together in harmony and understanding, for they were all children of one father.

But shortly afterwards Alexander died suddenly at Babylon, in 323 BC, not yet 33 years old. The world was shaken to its foundations. Demosthenes of Athens, orator and champion of freedom, a fierce opponent of Macedonia, tried to organise an insurrection in Greece, came to grief, fled, and took his own life with poison.

Opposite: A pass near Adana, occupying a key strategic position in relation to the Taurus Mountains; the troops of Alexander the Great marched on roads such as this
Right: Late Hellenistic statue of Alexander, from Magnesia ad Sipylum (Istanbul Museum)

Seleucus Nicator, one of the bravest and most prudent of Alexander's generals, seized the whole of the Near East for himself, and founded the empire of the Seleucids, which stretched from the Indus to the Mediterranean. Ptolemy, without doubt the most gifted and successful of Alexander's leaders and a relative of the great king, calmly helped himself to Egypt with its chief city of Alexandria and founded the dynasty of the Ptolemies, which lasted three hundred years until the quarrels with Rome under Cleopatra brought it to a close.

'By founding Alexandria,' said Napoleon, 'Alexander achieved more fame than with all his brilliant victories. This is the city that had to become the heart of the world.' Alexandria became the centre of world

Alexander the Great fighting the Persians in battle – detail from the sculptured reliefs on the 'Alexander sarcophagus', which was found at Sidon in the Lebanon and dates from about 320 BC (Istanbul Museum)

Aqueduct at Issus, where Alexander the Great won the battle against the Persians in 333 BC

trade. All the shipping routes and caravan trails began and ended there. The city became a melting-pot for men, races and civilisations. Here gathered atheists banished from the liberal and democratic city of Athens, believers from the Ganges, monotheistic Jews, and blasphemers from Asia Minor. Greek taste and eastern splendour were combined in a Greco-Egyptian style. A new moral world was created here. From now on, man and human knowledge held the centre of the stage.

Ptolemy I founded the museum of Alexandria, where the exact sciences of mathematics and physics were fostered. Adjoining the museum were botanical and zoological gardens, astronomical observatories with stone quadrants, astrolabes, armillary spheres and telescopes, a school of anatomy with equipment for

dissecting the human body, and finally the largest collection of books in the world.

The foundations of all mathematical sciences were laid down by Euclid in his *Elementa Matheseos*. Apollonius of Perga, the 'great geometer', wrote an epoch-making work on conic sections of which the methods are still valid today. The first calculation of the size of the earth was made by Eratosthenes, who was only fifty miles out in his estimate of its diameter. The first astronomical chart, a catalogue of the stars, calculations of the distances between sun, moon and earth, and the use of longitude and latitude were all worked out by Hipparchus of Nicaea. The manufacture of machines, including a steam engine, was described by Hero. The great doctor Herophilus from Chalcedon

City gate at Gordium, where Alexander the Great cut the Gordian Knot with his sword – it was said that whoever unloosed it would gain the mastery of Asia

developed medicine as an empirical science, and the foundations of anatomy, to replace the religious-based medicine that had so far prevailed. The movement of the earth around the sun and its own axis was first taught by Aristarchus of Samos.

Euclid's pupil, Archimedes of Syracuse, developed the theory of mechanics and hydrostatics, and invented the pulley-block and the water screw. Callimachus, head of the library at Alexandria, was the polymath of his time, exerting the widest influence with his writings and his lectures.

Every age and culture gropes for its appropriate form of self-expression – for its symbol. For Alexandria, the day of the great temples and mysteries was over, the time of the royal tombs was past, the age of absolute rule by

Below: En route to the oasis of Siwa, where in 332 BC Alexander the Great was hailed by the oracle as the son of the god Ammon (identified by the Greeks with Zeus)
Bottom: Map of Alexandria's harbours, engraved in 1699 (Greco-Roman Museum, Alexandria)
Opposite: Plaque carried by a priest of Ammon and featuring three Egyptian deities – black granite (Cairo Museum)

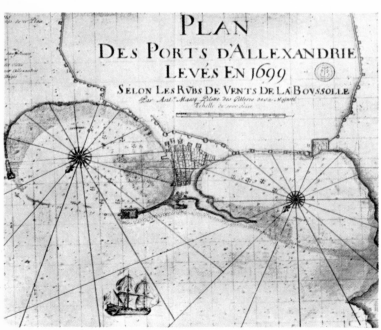

Below: The 'hall of the hundred columns' in the Apadana at Persepolis; the palace was burnt down by Alexander the Great in retaliation for the destruction of Athens by the Persians
Bottom: The River Tigris at Opis, where Alexander the Great held his great peace festival in 324 BC after his Indian campaign

the gods was finished, the power of the seers and poets was gone. The mysterious proportions that had governed beauty were outworn.

Man and man's reason, his determination to explore the things of this world and bend them to his will, became the supreme law. The new wonder of this world was the Pharos of Alexandria – a triumph of technology and to this day the archetype of every lighthouse in the world.

Probably already planned by Alexander the Great when the city was being designed, the lighthouse was not begun until about 300 BC under Ptolemy Soter, and was completed after twenty years' work in about 279 under Ptolemy Philadelphus, the second ruler of the Ptolemaic dynasty. The World Wonder stood on the peninsula of

Pharos, exactly where Qait Bay Fort stands today, which was built in about 1480 AD by the Mameluke sultan Qait Bay. The lighthouse took the name of the island, which was how it came to be called the Pharos of Alexandria.

The ancient foundations of the Pharos, although washed over by the sea, are still clearly distinguishable. Remains of the old lighthouse still lie in the water. There are a few granite blocks from the Pharos framing the doorway of the fort, broken stumps of old columns have been incorporated in the castle walls, and there is one capital to recall the former splendour of the World Wonder. Even in ancient times the island was linked to the mainland by a three-quarter-mile-long causeway, which in the course of time has been gradually widened

Below left: Head of a man, a miniature of the Hellenistic period (Greco-Roman Museum, Alexandria)
Below right: Hellenistic-age statue in black granite of an Egyptian scribe, found at Alexandria (Cairo Museum)
Bottom left: Head of a man in black basalt, Hellenistic period (Greco-Roman Museum, Alexandria)

Opposite: Statue of a woman which clearly displays a mixture of Greek and Egyptian styles (Qom Esh-Shuqafa catacombs, Alexandria)

Below: Head of a Greek priestess with Egyptian hair-style and head-ornament, about 250 BC (Greco-Roman Museum, Alexandria)

until today there is a whole district of the town situated on it.

The Alexandrian coins from imperial Roman times feature the lighthouse over and over again, either alone or with Isis, its protecting goddess. Comparisons with other illustrations and with the written accounts given in various different periods enable the appearance of the Pharos to be re-established beyond question. It consisted of three storeys. The lowest section was formed by a four-sided structure tapering slightly towards the top and reaching a height of 234 feet, and was half as wide as it was high. At the four corners, facing the four quarters of the wind and blowing conches, sat Tritons, sons of the sea-god Poseidon. The second of the receding stages was octagonal in shape

and, with its height of 113 feet, was about half as tall as the first storey. The third stage, again receding, was cylindrical in shape and thirty feet high. It housed the open fire providing the light which, gathered by a large concave mirror, could be seen from a distance of thirty-five miles. It is said, but not confirmed, that this device was attributable to Archimedes, and could also be used to set fire to enemy ships.

The Pharos was surmounted by a colossal figure, probably made of bronze and presumably representing Alexander, the founder of the city, or Ptolemy Soter, the first ruler of the empire, in the guise of the sun-god Helios. The building as a whole was protected from the sea by a walled platform.

Part of the causeway linking the island with the

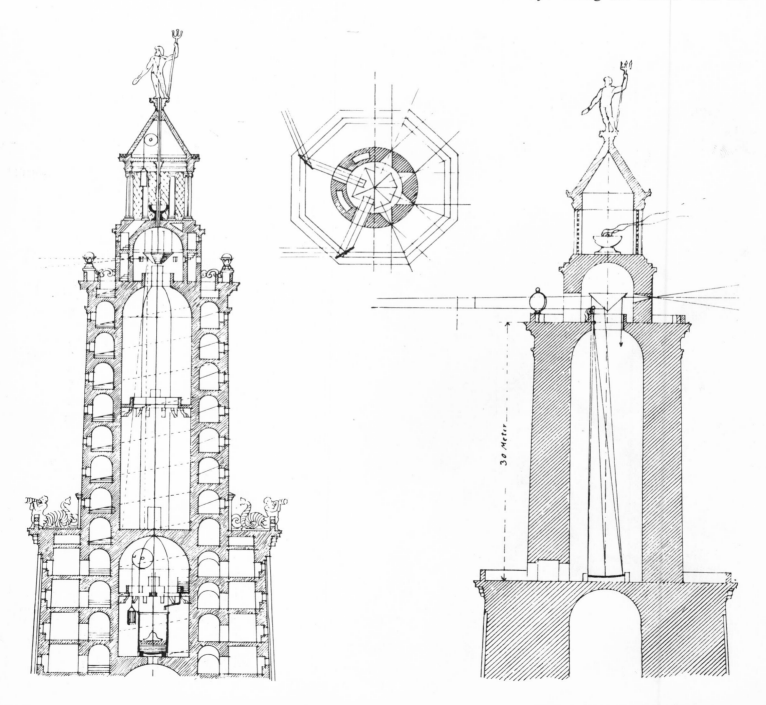

mainland was made into an aqueduct for bringing in drinking-water, which was stored in the bottom section of the lighthouse.

The internal arrangement of the Pharos, as described in the various reports that have been handed down to us, is echoed to a striking degree by the interior of the Qait Bay Fort. The square, octagonal and cylindrical shapes are retained on the inside of the building. Access to the top was provided within the tower by a wide and gently-sloping ramp that led upwards in a series of low landings. A shaft running from top to bottom served as a kind of lift for articles of every kind, not least the fuel for the fire. The many rooms around the periphery of the tower were reached by doorways leading off from the ramp, and had windows facing outwards. They were, of

The Qait Bay Fort at Alexandria, seen from the south

course, used for keeping a watch out to sea, but were certainly also employed by Alexandria's famous astronomers and mathematicians for their studies and experiments.

The design and construction of the Pharos is traditionally ascribed to 'Sostratus of Cnidus, son of Dexiphanes', who made a reputation as a highly gifted and versatile man with other projects besides this one, such as the Nile improvements at Memphis.

Among the famous copies made in ancient times of the Alexandrian Pharos – in the Roman port of Ostia, in Constantinople and Boulogne, for instance – the only one surviving is the 'Tower of Hercules' in La Coruña on the north-west corner of Spain, built by the Spaniard Servius Lupus in about 100 AD under the emperor

Trajan. Despite restoration at various times it retains its original shape and has been in continuous operation since the days of the emperor Trajan. We know the names of the men who have succeeded one another in the post of lighthouse-keeper, and we know that its light, constructed on the same principles as that of the Pharos of Alexandria, albeit somewhat modernised, has guided ships for almost two thousand years. Even if the pharos at La Coruña is not a complete replica of its predecessor, the World Wonder, and does not match its grandeur, it nonetheless gives us an idea of how extraordinary the original must have been.

When, around the middle of the first century BC, Egypt and the Ptolemaic empire became a battleground for Rome in its rise to world power, the Pharos

Opposite: Pompey's Pillar (eighty-eight feet high, eight feet ten inches in diameter at the base) and the colossal sphinx at Alexandria; Pompey is supposed to have been buried here
Right: The 'Torre de Hercules' at La Coruña on the north-west coast of Spain; built originally at the time of the emperor Trajan, it is the only lighthouse to have survived from antiquity

Opposite: High relief of the Egyptian goddess Isis – her features are entirely Greek (Cairo Museum)
Below: Relief on a sarcophagus; both the style and the figures portrayed are a clear mixture of Greek and Egyptian (Istanbul Museum)

of Alexandria remained unshaken. In the year 48 the once-mighty Pompey was murdered in Egypt while fleeing from his great enemy Julius Caesar, and is said to have been buried in Alexandria. Whatever the case, the enormous column known as Pompey's Pillar, built on ancient Egyptian foundations, testifies to the dead man's greatness. Cleopatra, the last of the Ptolemies, was then set up over her opponents by Caesar on a throne that depended on the favour of Rome. The famous library of Alexandria went up in flames – a catastrophe in itself and a disturbing symbol of the changing times.

After the Roman consul Mark Antony, ruler of the east since Caesar's assassination and the lover of Cleopatra, committed suicide at Alexandria with

Cleopatra following his defeat in the sea-battle of Actium (31 BC) at the hands of Caesar's nephew and successor Octavian, the focal point of the world shifted from Alexandria to Rome. But while this world empire faded away in its turn, the Pharos of Alexandria remained unchanged until the end of the eighth century AD. In the year 796 it was badly shaken by an earthquake. The Turks, the new masters of Egypt, tried to preserve it. However, at the turn of the eleventh and twelfth centuries the lighthouse was converted into a two-storey building surmounted by a mosque. A hundred years later the Pharos lay in ruins, until finally, in 1477, there arose from the rubble and the fragments the fortress which has survived substantially to our own day.

Below: Colossal head of Queen Cleopatra (Greco-Roman Museum, Alexandria)
Opposite: Colossal head of Mark Antony, found at Alexandria (Greco-Roman Museum, Alexandria)
Overleaf: Washed over by the sea, the rocks on which the Pharos of Alexandria was founded – a view from the top of Qait Bay Fort

Time Chart

Greece

1100–900: The great migration in the Mediterranean region, beginning of the Iron Age in Greece, period of the first colonies; settlements on the west coast of Asia Minor, emergence of the Greek alphabet

800–700: The Homeric epics and the *Odyssey,* composed of Greece into small com Delphic Oracle established, Games founded

c. 750: Unific Athens

Babylonia and Assyria

c. 4000: Federation of city-states in Sumer and Akkad

4000–3000: First dynasties of Kish, Uruk and Ur

c. 2500: Dynasty of Lagash

2414–2358: Sargon of Akkad (Sumer and Akkad united)

c. 2150: Gudea of Lagash

c. 2100: Third dynasty of Ur (Ur-nammu, Shulgi)

1793–1750: Hammurabi (founding of the Old Babylonian kingdom)

c. 1600: Hittite domination of Babylon

c. 1594: Kassite domination of Babylon

c. 1100: The Assyrians under Tiglath-pileser I conquer Babylon

883–859: Ashurnasirpal II

859–824: Shalmaneser III

809–782: Adad-nirari III (son of Semiramis, to whom the 'H Gardens' are traditionally ascri

745–727: Tigla

722–705:

704–6

Egypt

5000–4000: Neolithic age
Lower Egypt: Merimde-Benisalaam culture
Upper Egypt: Tasa culture

from 4000: Copper age
Cultures of Badari, Naqada I and Naqada II

c. 2900–2700: Early Dynastic period Agricultural civilisation, population of Hamitic–African origin, rule of the first and second dynasties, union of Upper and Lower Egypt under King Narmer (Menes is probably a name for the same king)

c. 2700: Founding of the Old Kingdom under King Zoser, building of the step pyramid and burial complex of Saqqara by the architect Imhotep

1 *2590–2469:* Rule of the fourth dynasty, age of the pyramid-builders, construction of the Great Pyramids at Giza under Kings Cheops, Chephren and Mycerinus

c. 2160: Breaking up of the Old Kingdom

| 4000 | 3000 | 2000 | 1000 | 900 | 800 | 700 |

546: Asia Minor conquered by the Persians

c. 513: First European campaign of Darius

500: Ionian revolt against Persia

c. 500–450: 'Early classical' period: Aeschylus, Pindar, building of the temple of Zeus at Olympia

490: Battle of Marathon: Athenian victory over the Persians

480: Second expedition to Greece of the Persians under Xerxes; battle of Thermopylae, Greek sea-victory at Salamis, Athens becomes a great power

449, 448: Persian wars ended, peace established with Persia

3 *c. 435–420:* Statue of Zeus of Olympia built by Phidias

431–404: The Peloponnesian War

386: The so-called King's peace, enforced between Sparta and the Greeks by the Persian king

356: Birth of Alexander the Great; temple of Artemis at Ephesus burnt down

4 *c. 356:* After the destruction of the older temple, work begins on the Artemision at Ephesus

5 Building of the Mausoleum at Halicarnassus

336: Assassination of Philip II; his son Alexander assumes power

332: Unopposed conquest of Egypt, Alexander's journey to the temple of Ammon in the Siwa oasis, foundation of Alexandria

331: Darius III defeated at Gaugamala, capture of Persepolis

327–325: Alexander's invasion of India

323: Death of Alexander at Babylon, division of his empire, commencement of the Hellenistic dynasties under Alexander's former commanders (the Diadochi); Ptolemy Soter founds the Ptolemaic dynasty in Egypt, with Alexandria as capital

Ashurbanipal

₅25: Establishment of the neo-Babylonian kingdom under Nabopolassar (625–605)

2 *605–562:* Nebuchadnezzar II (rebuilding of the city of Babylon and construction of the Hanging Gardens)

587: Destruction of Jerusalem

539: Cyrus II of Persia conquers Babylon, end of the neo-Babylonian kingdom and of the political independence of Mesopotamia

6 *c. 300–280:* Building of the Colossus of Rhodes

7 Building of the Pharos of Alexandria

600   500   400   300   200   100   0 AD

Index and Glossary